Scotland
and its regions

ABERDEEN AND GRAMPIAN
Aberdeen
ANGUS AND DUNDEE
Dundee
FIFE
North Berwick
Dunfermline
EDINBURGH AND THE LOTHIANS
Edinburgh
SCOTTISH BORDERS
Hawick
ENGLAND
PERTHSHIRE
Perth
Stirling
Linlithgow
GLASGOW AND CLYDE VALLEY
Glasgow
Dumfries
DUMFRIES AND GALLOWAY
AYRSHIRE AND ARRAN
Ayr
ARRAN
Campbeltown
Stranraer
HIGHLANDS AND SKYE
Inverness
Fort William
Oban
ARGYLL
JURA
ISLAY
COLONSAY
MULL
COLL
TIREE
SKYE
Uig
Portree
RUM
EIGG
MUCK
CANNA
BARRA
BENBECULA
SOUTH UIST
NORTHERN IRELAND

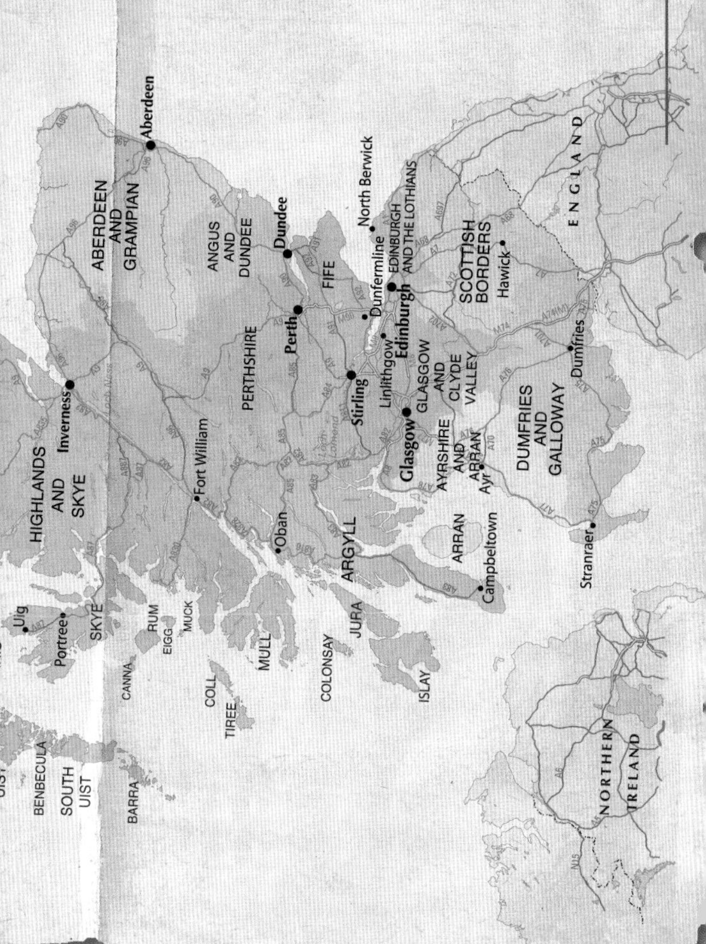

Contents
Overview & by Region

Loch Scavaig, Skye

2-3 ....Introduction
6-10 ....Facts and Figures

REGIONS
12-15 ....Shetland
16-19 ....Orkney
20-23 ....The Outer Hebrides
24-29 ....Highlands & Skye
30-35 ....Aberdeen & Grampian
36-40 ....Angus & Dundee
41-45 ....Perthshire
46-51 ....Argyll, the Isles, Loch Lomond, Stirling and Trossachs
52-56 ....The Kingdom of Fife
57-61 ....Edinburgh & the Lothians
62-67 ....Glasgow & the Clyde Valley
68-72 ....Ayrshire & Arran
73-79 ....Dumfries & Galloway
80-84 ....Scottish Borders

85-94 ....Local Listings
95-110 .....Calendar of Events

111-117 ...Top Ten Must Sees
120...........Getting to Scotland
122-131 ...Directory of Visitor Information Centres
132-133 ...Competition
134-136 ...Notes

Published 2008 | Text © VisitScotland 2008 | Photography © Scottish Viewpoint
Design by Frame Ltd | All rights reserved | This guide is printed on recycled content paper.

VisitScotland is committed to ensuring that our environment, upon which our tourism is so dependent, is safe guarded for future generations to enjoy.

ISBN 0-85419-695-1

SHETLAND
Lerwick
ORKNEY
Kirkwall
Thurso
OUTER
HEBRIDES
Stornoway

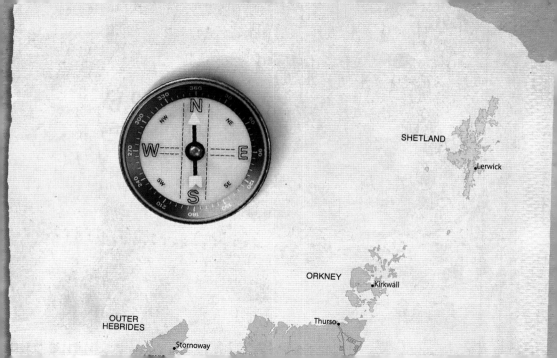

DUNKELD, PERTHSHIRE

Contents
by Activity

Arts/museums 19, 23, 26, 33, 34, 37, 38, 39, 40, 42, 45, 54, 55, 56, 61, 63, 71, 77

Beaches........ 14, 15, 17, 21, 22, 25, 28, 34, 38, 40, 49, 70, 72, 75

Castles, Cathedrals and Historic Houses 18, 31, 32, 33, 35, 37, 38, 51, 53, 55, 59, 61, 69, 70, 71, 74, 78, 81, 82, 83

Events and Festivals 15, 35, 61, 63, 95-110

Excursions/walks......... 13, 17, 18, 21, 22, 23, 25, 26, 27, 28, 31, 34, 37, 38, 42, 43, 44, 47, 48, 49, 53, 63, 66, 71, 72, 74, 76, 81

Food and Drink................. 15, 19, 23, 27, 29, 31, 33, 34, 39, 40, 42, 43, 45, 49, 56, 58, 59, 60, 61, 63, 64, 65, 66, 67, 69, 70, 72, 77, 78, 79, 84, 85-94 (listings)

Golf...47, 56, 84, 89

Great views 13, 17, 18, 21, 25, 26, 27, 37, 42, 43, 47, 51, 58, 70, 71, 75, 76, 77, 81, 82, 83

Historical spots.......13, 14, 17, 18, 19, 21, 22, 31, 37, 38, 42, 49, 53, 54, 55, 56, 60, 61, 63, 67, 69, 70, 71, 72, 76, 77, 83

Parks & Gardens ...28, 32, 37, 43, 44, 45, 58, 59, 64, 74, 75, 78, 82

Rivers & Lochs.............28, 31, 37, 45, 48, 49, 50, 51, 63, 65, 71, 76

Where to stay..85-94 (listings)

Wildlife watching......................14, 18, 25, 26, 27, 28, 29, 31, 32, 35, 47, 60, 63, 64, 71, 77, 79, 81, 82, 84

For even more information, go to www.visitscotland.com/perfectday

Introduction
A warm welcome

Bass Rock from North Berwick

Old Tolbooth Wynd, Edinburgh

WELCOME *to the Scotland you may not have seen before.*

It's no secret that the best way to enjoy a place is to get the inside track from the people who live there.

In our hunt for the best of Scotland, we've asked people from all over the country to give us their best ideas and recommendations.

Scotland's main visitor sites are already easy to find, so this is no ordinary guide book: we've gone with the personal, the opinionated and definitely not the run of the mill.

We hope you'll enjoy dipping into this special, limited edition guide. We've called it ***'Real Scotland – the Locals' Guide'****. It's your passport to new places.*

Glen Affric, Highlands

PASSENGER
E MCDO.
FROM
LDN
TO
EDI

Flight	Date
BE7321	06JUN

Gate	Time	Seat
8	1150	27A

Discover the silent secrets
of the hidden Highland Spring.

Facts & figures

Did you know?

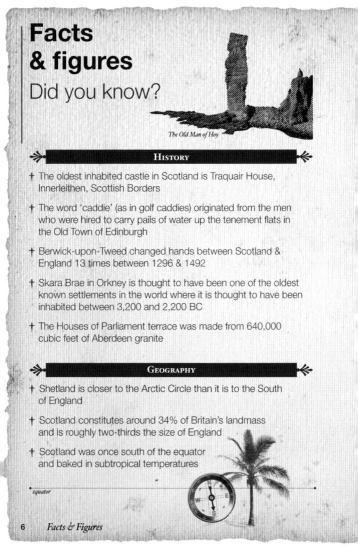

The Old Man of Hoy

History

- The oldest inhabited castle in Scotland is Traquair House, Innerleithen, Scottish Borders
- The word 'caddie' (as in golf caddies) originated from the men who were hired to carry pails of water up the tenement flats in the Old Town of Edinburgh
- Berwick-upon-Tweed changed hands between Scotland & England 13 times between 1296 & 1492
- Skara Brae in Orkney is thought to have been one of the oldest known settlements in the world where it is thought to have been inhabited between 3,200 and 2,200 BC
- The Houses of Parliament terrace was made from 640,000 cubic feet of Aberdeen granite

Geography

- Shetland is closer to the Arctic Circle than it is to the South of England
- Scotland constitutes around 34% of Britain's landmass and is roughly two-thirds the size of England
- Scotland was once south of the equator and baked in subtropical temperatures

equator

Tallest & Highest

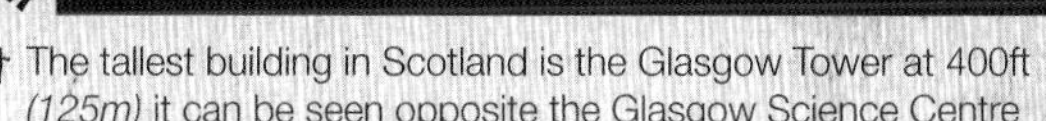

- † The tallest building in Scotland is the Glasgow Tower at 400ft *(125m)* it can be seen opposite the Glasgow Science Centre near the River Clyde
- † The world's highest beech hedge can be found in Meikleour, Perthshire measuring 100ft *(30m)* tall (and 1/3 mile long!)
- † Scotland's highest mountain is Ben Nevis at a height of 4,406ft *(1,344m)*
- † The highest village in Scotland is Wanlockhead in Dumfriesshire at 1,411ft *(430m)*
- † A Yew tree in Fortingall churchyard (North of Loch Tay) is over 3,000 years old
- † The tallest sea-stack in Britain is the Old Man of Hoy, Orkney at 450ft *(137m)*

Scotland's Major Populations

Glasgow	c600,000
Edinburgh	c450,000
Highlands	c218,000
Aberdeen	c210,000
Dundee	c140,000

Lochs & Waterways

- † Loch Lomond is the largest stretch of fresh water in mainland Britain (27sq miles); Loch Ness has the biggest volume of water in Scotland (7 billion cubic metres of water), while Loch Morar is the deepest at 1,077ft (328m)
- † Scotland's longest river is the River Tay measuring nearly 120 miles in length
- † There are 40 mainland sea lochs in Scotland

Facts & figures

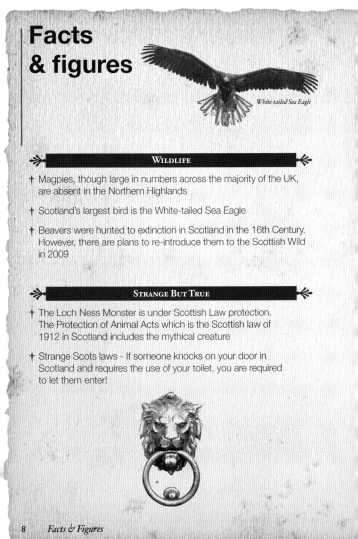

White-tailed Sea Eagle

Wildlife

- Magpies, though large in numbers across the majority of the UK, are absent in the Northern Highlands
- Scotland's largest bird is the White-tailed Sea Eagle
- Beavers were hunted to extinction in Scotland in the 16th Century. However, there are plans to re-introduce them to the Scottish Wild in 2009

Strange But True

- The Loch Ness Monster is under Scottish Law protection. The Protection of Animal Acts which is the Scottish law of 1912 in Scotland includes the mythical creature
- Strange Scots laws - If someone knocks on your door in Scotland and requires the use of your toilet, you are required to let them enter!

How Long a Kilt Should Be

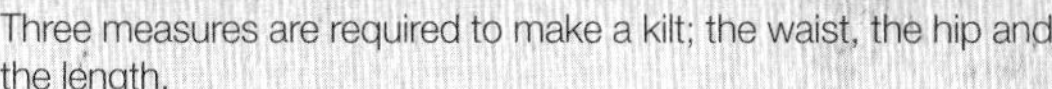

Three measures are required to make a kilt; the waist, the hip and the length.

A kilt should fit from just sufficiently above the waist to allow a belt to be worn, to the centre of the knee.

Use the table of lengths given below as a guide:

Height	5'4" *(163cm)*	5'6" *(168cm)*	5'8" *(173cm)*	5'10" *(178cm)*	6' *(183cm)*	6'2" *(188cm)*
Kilt length	21¼" *(54cm)*	22" *(56cm)*	22¾" *(58cm)*	23½" *(60cm)*	24¼" *(62cm)*	25" *(64cm)*

A Guide to First Footing

Usually the New Year is brought in at home and then one 'first foots' round friends who are keeping an open house. A small gift is taken to 'hansel' the house - a piece of coal for the fire or, in some communities, a red herring, or some shortbread. The coal ensures that the house will always be warm and safe, and the food ensures that the household will never be hungry through the year.

After twelve midnight has struck, the gentlemen have the right to kiss all the ladies present. It is considered very lucky for the first person to cross the threshold after midnight to be a man, well built, dark and handsome. As many as fifty people could pass through an open house in the course of the morning and there is eating of black bun, shortbread, cold delicacies and even more drinking of uisge beatha (Water of Life – Whisky).

It is traditional also for old things in the house to be thrown out and women can still be seen scrubbing their doorsteps just before twelve to welcome in the New Year. The greeting from those stepping into the house is:

A Guid New Year to ane and a'
And mony may ye see.

Facts & figures

 **BURNS SUPPER PROTOCOL** 

The format can be whatever the organiser wishes. As for the poems used, the 'Address to the Haggis' is essential - verses 1, 2, 3 and 8. The other poems used reflect the kind of personnel attending the Supper. Some functions have guest orators who might offer Tam o' Shanter, Holy Willie's Prayer (with actions) or The Cottar's Saturday Night. Some Burns Clubs do indulge in guest orators as they feel Robert Burns' poems were meant to be read aloud if necessary but not acted.

The menu may be as you please but traditionally, it is as follows:

† Soup such as Cock-a-Leekie or Scotch Broth

† Haggis, Champit Tatties (mashed potatoes) and Neeps (mashed turnip)

† Bannocks an' Kebbuck (cheese - such as the hard cheeses of Mull, Galloway or Orkney, biscuits and oatcakes)

There is always whisky to toast the Immortal Memory with a dram for the piper who pipes in the ceremonial haggis carried by the chef for the 'Address to the Haggis'. Whisky is normally available throughout the Supper.

For more information on Homecoming 2009 which celebrates the 250th anniversary of the birth of Robert Burns, go to www.homecomingscotland2009.com

The Regions

What to see and do region by region

Shetland
Hidden secrets

LERWICK HARBOUR

AN *archipelago that lies below the horizon as seen from the mainland, Shetland is definitely different and feels more 'abroad' than anywhere else in Britain. Sometimes described as a crossroads on the northern seas, it is certainly cosmopolitan. Shetland does not occupy a box at the side of the UK map – instead it's in a northern world of its own. With wildlife spectacles and grand seascapes terminating every view, and with their Scandinavian links, heritage and a vibrant culture, the Shetland folk are comfortable with their sense of community. And they know how to make music at parties... in short, this is a destination for the adventurous.*

Cliffs at Eshaness

UNMISSABLE

Eshaness

Wild seascapes and weird stacks offshore make this drive west of Hillswick a must. Take the lighthouse road for a walk north, to the Holes of Scraada (the names are as surreal as the scenery). But remember, this is rugged and challenging country - take care.

Muckle Flugga

Go to the top of Shetland? Definitely. It's an undemanding hike up Hermaness Hill with a brilliant view to Muckle Flugga. Keep to the path though. It's a national nature reserve and the skuas can be aggressive! (Hold your hand above your head as you walk if you're anxious. It looks silly but keeps the birds higher.) **www.snh.org.uk**

Broch at Mousa

Icons of the north, brochs are mysterious structures scattered around in various states of ruin. Mousa Broch is in an exceptionally complete state and absolutely fascinating. It's on a wee island – so you'll have to book your excursion. **www.mousaboattrips.co.uk**

The Monk's Stone, Lerwick

Spot an Otter

WORTH A LOOK

St Ninian's Isle

Famous for the finding of Pictish treasure, St Ninian's Isle is anchored to the mainland by a tombolo, a back-to-back beach. Your picnic place will depend which way the wind blows! Loch of Spiggie nature reserve is close by.

A Viking industrial site

Sometimes overlooked as visitors go to high profile places like Jarlshof, by Cunningsburgh, the Catpund Burn (stream) was where the Vikings made their crockery! A few minutes walk upstream reveals obvious work sites, where the soapstone vessels were literally cut from the soft rock. Some are still there in an unfinished state.

Spot an otter

The road up to the lighthouse at Sumburgh Head gives easy viewing of puffins – that's well known (they're just over the wall). But this is also a good place to see otters. Keep a sharp look out along the foot of the cliffs (summer nights are best). Highest otter population in the UK is in Shetland.

St Ninian's Isle

More to explore

Most northerly

Collect loads of 'most northerlies' on Unst – road, house, post-office, hotel – even brewery! Plus there's a well furnished bus shelter near Haroldswick with carpets, curtains, TV etc – probably the most surreal sight in Shetland.

Burra

More beaches here – Meal and Banna Min are amongst the very best on the island, easily accessible from Lerwick.

Inter-island ferries

Efficient and surprisingly inexpensive, but book in advance in main season. Run by Shetland Islands Council.
www.shetland.gov.uk/ferries

Shetland Folk Festival

Long established and most northerly in the UK (inevitably!) with huge prestige on the folk circuit. Though headline artistes perform, local musicians also demonstrate stunning quality.
www.shetlandfolkfestival.com

Monty's Bistro

Found in the wynds of Lerwick port, great place for local lamb and seafood.
www.eatscotland.com

Orkney
Hidden secrets

Whalebone, Birsay

Cross *from Scrabster on mainland Scotland and the first impressions of Orkney are misleading, as the ferry sails below the wild and massive sandstone cliffs of Hoy. Only as the bows swing east into Scapa Flow will you see that the prevailing colour is green and surprisingly soft. This archipelago with its good grazing has supported a population of farmers and sea-rovers for thousands of years. There are more prehistoric sites here than anywhere else in the UK, with Skara Brae a quite extraordinary survivor. The other surprise is the quality of the shopping along Kirkwall's main street – in particular local jewellery, knitwear and crafts.*

Old Man of Hoy

UNMISSABLE

Skara Brae

You can actually imagine yourself living in these dwellings with their stone furniture. Yet the last inhabitants moved out more than 4,000 years ago. You'll never be closer to Stone Age life. Make time for a beach walk here as well. **www.historic-scotland.gov.uk**

Old Man of Hoy from Rackwick Bay

From the Orkney ferry, the Old Man of Hoy is awesome, yet dwarfed by the scale of the nearby cliffs. For a closer look, take path from Rackwick Bay. NB. Keep on path – great skuas (bonxies) breed nearby and will dive-bomb! This excursion is possible as a day trip using Hoy ferry, which takes cars – but you've got to be a brisk walker!

Looking for initials at the Ring of Brodgar

Set between water and sky, the standing stones of the Ring of Brodgar date from the 3rd millennium BC. Most visitors stroll round. Instead, examine the broken stones; on one of them, sometime in the 12th century, a bored Viking carved his name in runes on its inner side. He was called Bjorn. **www.historic-scotland.gov.uk**

Yesnaby

Magnificent seascapes here. Walk south for dramatic coastline. The rare Primula scotica (Scots primrose) grows on the coastal heath nearby. The square areas of concrete on the cliff edge here are remains of wartime defences and gun batteries protecting Scapa Flow.

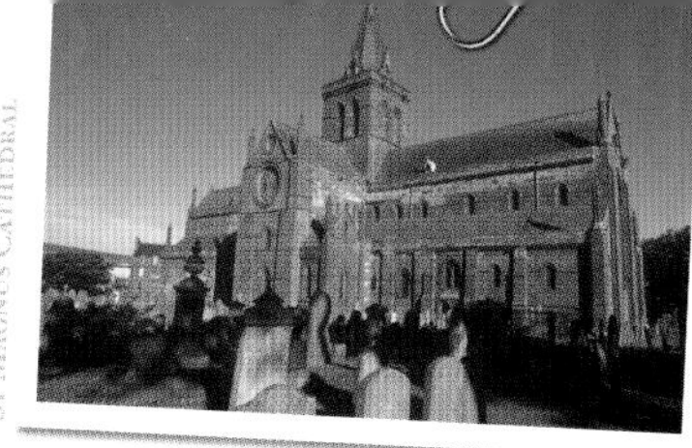
St Magnus Cathedral

WORTH A LOOK

View of St Magnus Cathedral

St Magnus Cathedral is both magnificent and unexpected in these northlands. For a good overview, visit the Bishop's Palace opposite and look across from the top of its 16th-century tower. From this vantage point the sheer scale of the work can be appreciated. **www.historic-scotland.gov.uk | www.stmagnus.org.uk**

Can you see Fair Isle?

Wideford Hill is just west of Kirkwall. Well worth the drive to the top because summer sunsets sometimes light up the distant cliffs of Fair Isle, away to the north. And from Fair Isle you can see Shetland. Suddenly, you're a Viking, navigating home…

Kitchener Memorial at Marwick Head

Hold your hat on tightly - this has to be the windiest place in Orkney! Poignant tower recalling the loss of HMS Hampshire nearby, with Lord Kitchener aboard. From carpark walk uphill, then south for best views of seabird colony. Cliffs with seabirds (RSPB Reserve) and memorial tower best photographed in the afternoon, when the sun comes round.

Maeshowe and the Dragon

The famous Maeshowe dragon symbol is a recurring Orcadian theme. The original is inside the ancient burial mound of Maeshowe, along with a large amount of Viking runic graffiti. But can you persuade the guide to translate the rude bits? **www.historic-scotland.gov.uk**

More to explore

DISCOUNT ADMISSIONS
USE A HISTORIC SCOTLAND REGIONAL EXPLORER PASS FOR ORKNEY – THERE ARE SO MANY SITES THAT THE SAVINGS ON ADMISSION ARE REALLY WORTHWHILE.
WWW.HISTORIC-SCOTLAND.GOV.UK

ROVING EYE TOUR
SEE LAST RESTING PLACE OF SCUTTLED GERMAN WWI FLEET IN SCAPA BY ON-BOARD GUIDED TOUR WITH ROVING EYE ENTERPRISES. THEY USE UNDERWATER REMOTE-CONTROLLED VEHICLE (ROV) FOR AMAZING PICTURES.

WORLD'S SHORTEST SCHEDULED FLIGHT.
INTER-ISLAND: WESTRAY TO PAPA WESTRAY, ABOUT TWO MINUTES. OLDEST DWELLINGS IN EUROPE NEAR AIRFIELD – 5000-YEAR-OLD HOUSES AT KNAP OF HOWAR.

PIER ARTS CENTRE
CHECK OUT LATEST CULTURAL OFFERINGS HERE ON THE HARBOURFRONT AT STROMNESS. RECENTLY REFURBISHED.

STROMNESS MUSEUM
INDEPENDENTLY RUN MUSEUM. FASCINATING MEMORABILIA FROM THE SCUTTLED GERMAN FLEET AND ALSO THE HUDSON BAY COMPANY.

VICTORIA RESTAURANT
BASED IN THE 17TH CENTURY ORKNEY HOTEL, TOP QUALITY CUISINE AND SERVICE.
WWW.EATSCOTLAND.COM

The Outer Hebrides

Hidden secrets

Calanais Standing Stones

A whole host of experiences are on offer as you explore this long chain of islands. For Lewis, beyond the main centre of Stornoway, its rolling miles of peatlands with prehistory galore, especially the iconic Standing Stones of Calanais. Harris is much more mountainous, while in the Uists and Benbecula wild nature seems all around, co-existing with the scattered population. The further south you go, the greater the sense of magical adventure. Though a Gaelic language heartland, everyone speaks English. But make no mistake, the west can certainly cast a spell – especially if the sun shines and the signature colour is that special greeny-blue where the beach slides under the wave.

Black House at Arnol.

UNMISSABLE

Princes Beach

Eriskay's local stores are nearby, so take a picnic to the little table above the Princes Beach on Eriskay (where Bonnie Prince Charlie landed.) Do nothing. Just gaze at the white sands. (Bring sunglasses.) Watch the Barra ferry depart and simply enjoy the view.

Black House at Arnol

You'll never complain about it being stuffy ever again after a visit to the Black House at Arnol. How did they cope with the peat smoke? Definitely the place in the Outer Hebrides to see how the local folk lived long ago. **www.historic-scotland.org.uk**

Traigh Luskentyre

Easy access to these dazzling sands from the main road, at the south end of the beach. Scenes from the feature film 'The Rocket Post' shot here, while other media point of interest is just offshore: Taransay, of BBC's Castaway fame.

Traigh Luskentyre

Butt of Lewis

WORTH A LOOK

Whale watching from the Butt of Lewis

Is it worth going all the way to the end of Lewis? Definitely – plenty to see on the way by way of ruined brochs, standing stones and other early sites, as well as craft outlets. And Port of Ness has a fine restaurant and a heritage centre. The lighthouse at the Butt is a good place to see whales.

SS Politician

Between Eriskay and South Uist, nothing visible now above the waves of the spot where the famous cargo of whisky went down. The site is on your left, well down the channel, as you drive to Eriskay on the causeway. The island's only pub has a rescued bottle on display and you can take your beer outside when the weather is fine.

Tolsta Beach

If time is limited, then Traigh Mhor ('big beach') by North Tolsta is an easy drive north-east from Stornoway. Though the beach stretches south from the road-end, if you walk the track a little way north, you'll see the 'Bridge to Nowhere' – a handsome concrete span, part of the abortive road-making plans of one-time island owner Lord Leverhulme.

See the plane arrive on the beach at Barra

Sure, plane-spotting is a bit corny – but this is different. The inter-island and Glasgow service lands on a huge sandy beach. There are various little vantage points on the airport road, just by the edge of the sands. (You can tell when a plane is due – the cockle pickers get out of the way!)

More to explore

Best coffee in South Uist

It may rain and if it does, then warm up with a proper coffee at the (very civilised) café in Hebridean Jewellery. There are beautiful hand-crafted jewellery pieces as well here, costing a little more than the coffee!

www.hebrideanjewellery.co.uk

St Kilda Day Trip

41 miles west of Benbecula. Boat from Leverburgh, Harris of Harris.

www.seaharris.co.uk

Boat trip to Mingulay

From Barra, watch the weather forecast and choose your day for a boat trip round uninhabited Mingulay. Spectacular cliffs over 600ft high on the west side.

www.nts.org.uk

Salmon sandwiches at toffee maker

Travel the length of the Western Isles and on Barra there's a toffee maker. Best of all, call at lunchtime and they'll make you the best ever hot-smoked salmon sandwiches. Then sit outside on benches and enjoy the view to Kisimul Castle.

www.hebrideantoffeecompany.com

Informal Ceilidh sessions at Lochboisdale Hotel.

The best-kept secret in the Uists. Sometimes the owner invites some musical friends round on a Friday and they just play. It's not for the benefit of guests at the hotel. No, they just like playing! Unplanned, instant ceilidh!

www.lochboisdale.com

Highlands & Skye

Hidden secrets

TORRIDON

The Highlands of Scotland have a special trick. They can be perceived as vast, remote, wild and hard to reach and at the same time be hospitable, hauntingly beautiful and easily accessible. It is as if they appeal to our need to connect with somewhere unspoilt – while still holding onto our home comforts! Best of all, they offer extraordinary diversity of landscape within a comparatively small area. From the Flow Country of the far north, via the ancient rocks of Torridon to the high plateau of the Cairngorms – it won't take too long to cover the ground – yet what treats for all the senses lie in store.

Morar Sands

UNMISSABLE

View the Cuillin from Elgol

The panorama looking towards the Skye Cuillin could be the finest mountain view in the UK. There are boat trips from here - but if you want to explore on foot, find the coastal path between two crofts (on the way downhill). But be careful, the track soon crosses a steep slope that ends in the sea below. Fabulous views – but you'll need a head for heights as well.

Search for otters at Plockton

Hoping to see an otter? Hire a rowing boat from Calum MacKenzie and gently make your way westwards round the point and keep your eyes open. Alternatively, if you go with his own guided boat trips then he will take you out to see seals. And if you don't see any, the trip is free! **www.calums-sealtrips.com**

Discover Achiltibuie

If you can take your eyes off the landscapes hereabouts, then the local Achiltibuie Smokehouse is a must for stocking up on classy Highland foodstuffs. Achnahaird Beach is another 'must see' on the peninsula. The views in all directions of this wild part of the north-west are magical.

The Silver Sands of Morar

The Silver Sands of Morar have iconic status – the essence of western seaboard. But you can still enjoy deserted stretches. Park at Tougal (or Toigal as some OS maps spell it) and walk out on the sands, on the south shore, where the River Morar meets the sea. Follow the sands round the headland to lose the crowds.

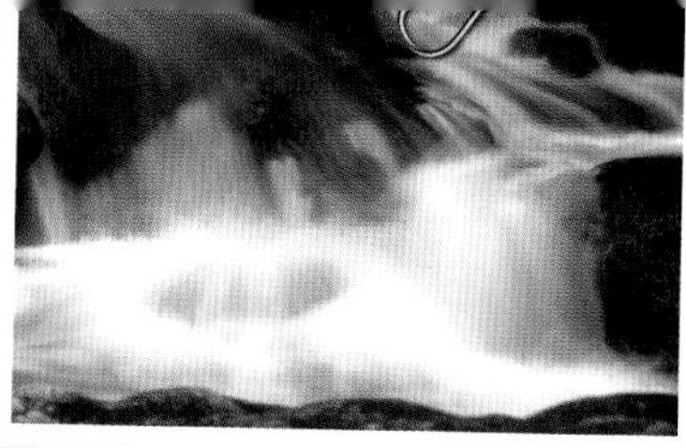

Steall Falls, Glen Nevis

WORTH A LOOK

Going to extremes 1 – Cape Wrath

To reach Cape Wrath, at the north-westerly tip, take the little ferry across the Kyle of Durness. A mini-bus will take you 11 miles to the lighthouse. It is possible to use this service for an expedition along the tops of Scotland's highest mainland sea cliffs. But for something much gentler, then stroll along Balnakeil beach near Durness. **Cape Wrath Information line (military range programme) freephone 0800 833 300**

Going to extremes 2 – Around John O' Groats

Park just by the Duncansby Head lighthouse. Stroll a short way across the rolling heath for a stunning view of the Stacks of Duncansby. Better still, head for the cliff edge north of the Stacks, and in a certain gully, have a close look at the grassy upper parts. You're sure to see seabirds up-close.

Going to extremes 3 – Ardnamurchan Point

It's worth going to the most westerly point in mainland Scotland. The views from the lighthouse are stunning and there is an exhibition with information on the area (and a little café) in the former lighthouse ancillary buildings. On the way, the Ardnamurchan Natural History Centre has a tearoom that does take-aways if you want to take provisions to explore the beaches on the north side of the peninsula.

The Glen behind the Ben

Leave the bustle of the Great Glen road and the town of Fort William behind and drive to the head of Glen Nevis. A 90 minute walk will take you to the spectacular Steall Falls (where the dragon scene was filmed in Harry Potter and the Goblet of Fire). There is also a challenging wire bridge for you to try if you have a head for heights.

Driftwood fire, Dores

Monster views

The road (B862) via the village of Dores down the east side of Loch Ness is an alternative to the main Inverness to Fort William trunk road. Good view from the beach at Dores. A glimpse of the mysterious beast is not guaranteed, but you should spot the resident spotter and his van. He's been there a long time (some say seventeen years) and makes little Nessie souvenirs to while away the hours!

A Scottish 'burgh'

Some towns have retained an old-established ambience. Visit Cromarty, on the Black Isle – an easy journey from Inverness. Stroll around and enjoy its fine 18th-century domestic architecture. Choice of places to eat – if you're on a budget the local baker has a good reputation. Take your savoury pie up to the South Sutor, the nearby headland, for sea views across the Firth.

See an eagle from the boat on Loch Sheil

A classic panorama: the view down Loch Sheil from Glenfinnan. Take a boat trip on the loch for a different perspective. And you might well see a Golden Eagle. Combine it with a pub lunch (at least) at the Glenfinnan Hotel nearby – excellent Scottish cooking. You can tell that by the number of locals who frequent it!
www.highlandcruises.co.uk www.glenfinnanhouse.com

Stac Polly

WORTH A LOOK *(continued)*

The Moray Firth's Dolphins

You can see dolphins from the Firth shore quite often - sometimes very close. Try Spey Bay, near Elgin, at the river mouth. The River Spey reaches the sea through a huge storm-beach of rounded grey stones. This is a great place for beach-combing, especially for twisty bits of branch and root, artfully smoothed by wind and water. Take away a tasteful souvenir – for free.

The Green Loch in the Cairngorms National Park

Lose the crowds by walking (or cycling) the track north-east beyond Glenmore Lodge, near Aviemore. Serious walkers also use it to reach lesser-known Cairngorm tops such as Bynack More. Follow it as far as An Lochan Uaine – in Gaelic, the little green loch. Shaded by trees but easily accessible from the track, it is a curious shade of bluey-green in all lights.

All aboard for the garden

If you had a home in an out-of-the-way part of the North-West Highlands, only accessible by boat, you might not think of building a garden and opening it to the public. But that's what's been done at Kerrachar Gardens, near the Kylseku Bridge. They open regularly during the summer months. Check website for opening and sailing times. No other garden quite like it. **www.kerrachar.co.uk**

More to explore

Sample whisky – then buy it!

In Craigellachie, the Whisky Bar at the Craigellachie Hotel has an awesome (and alphabetical) selection of over 700 different whiskies ranged on shelves right round the room. Meanwhile, Gordon and MacPhail is Elgin's main whisky shop. They have been selecting and bottling malt whiskies for generations and have remained independent and family owned.

www.craigellachie.co.uk

www.gordonandmacphail.com

Red deer by the road

Look out for them on the open moors by Loch Glascarnoch between Garve and Ullapool, except perhaps in high summer when they'll be higher on the hills.

Lochinver pies

Pies both savoury and sweet at the Lochinver Larder. They despatch pies far and wide, but you can sample them in this north-western village.

Scotland's Geoparks

There are two. Both in the Highlands. North West Highland Geopark all around the area north of Ullapool. Knockan Crag, by the main road between Ardmair and Ledmore has interpretative facilities. Lochaber Geopark includes highest mountain and deepest loch in Scotland.

www.northwest-highlands-geopark.org.uk

www.lochabergeopark.org.uk

Captain's Galley

Award-winning seafood specialist at Scrabster, ferry port for Orkney.

www.captainsgalley.co.uk

Aberdeen & Grampian

Hidden secrets

Musicians play harbourside, Portsoy

One *thing is for sure – the city of Aberdeen appeals to the senses in a way that's different from other Scottish cities. It's the colour of the granite, the sound of the gulls and the salt-smell of the sea for a start (and you could add, the taste of the freshest of seafood). It's a place that knows it's different: partly a large market town servicing the fertile, comfortable and mostly farming landscapes all around; partly a European oil centre of international importance. Ultimately, it's the North Sea that has shaped the city, both past and present. And even the down-to-earth accents and dialect throughout these northlands have their own smattering of words that tell of Scandinavian links. Yes, north-east Scotland may only be a couple of hours to the north – but it can feel like a different world.*

Dunnottar Castle

UNMISSABLE

Dunnottar Castle

Northbound, divert just before Stonehaven to visit Dunnottar Castle, a stand-in for Elsinore in the 1991 Hamlet with Mel Gibson. Built on a high fortified headland, ruined Dunnottar Castle is on an exposed spot. You may want to warm up afterwards. Stop off at Robertsons of Stonehaven, bakers in Allardyce Street. Their upstairs café serves authentic Scottish mince and tatties. **www.dunnottarcastle.co.uk**

Loch of Strathbeg

For a bare and forlorn ambience, this loch is hard to beat. Scotland's largest land-locked lagoon is a stopover for thousands of geese and ducks (RSPB reserve). Just the spot for some pure northern air. Afterwards, try the 'funcy pieces' (calorie laden baked cakes) at the Happy Plant Centre, Mintlaw.

Townhouse, City of Aberdeen

Crathes Castle Gardens

UNMISSABLE *(continued)*

Crathes Castle and Garden

Combine a pleasing castle with a stunning garden. While Crathes' interior features rare painted ceilings, the garden is designed as a series of rooms within close-clipped yew hedges. If you get a taste for castles, remember that all the fortresses on the Castle Trail are atmospheric but not all of them (unlike Crathes) have roofs! **www.nts.org.uk**

Red deer at Glen Muick

At the road-end in Glen Muick, near Ballater, there is a car park. Keep your finger hovering over the camera zoom button because by the nearby river-flats there should be red deer. And if you're prepared to walk a bit (actually, quite a bit), you'll see the Royal Family's hideaway of the Glas Alt Shiel at the far end of Loch Muick.

Loch Muick

Falconry display at Fyvie Castle

WORTH A LOOK

Fyvie Castle

The magnificently rambling five-towered Fyvie Castle is less than an hour's drive beyond Aberdeen. As is traditional, it has a curse, a secret chamber, and some ghosts. More importantly for the culturally inclined, it has a rich collection of mostly portraits by artists such as Batoni, Romney, Gainsborough, Opie, Lawrence and Hoppner, plus one of the largest private collections of Raeburns in the world. **www.nts.org.uk**

Proper seafood

Fishing is important in North-East Scotland. Good seafood restaurants include Eat on the Green at Pitmedden, The Silver Darling in Aberdeen, the Fjord Inn near Turriff. At the budget end, try award-winning fish and chip shops like the Bervie Chipper at Stonehaven and the Ashvale in Brechin. Tie in a visit to the Aberdeen Maritime Museum. **www.aagm.co.uk**

Stonehaven Harbour

Lighthouse Museum, Fraserburgh

WORTH A LOOK *(continued)*

To the Lighthouse

The Museum of Scottish Lighthouses at Fraserburgh, at Kinnaird Head on the very tip of North-East Scotland, is a great day out. As well as artefacts from lighthouses, the experience also takes in a real lighthouse, built on top of a 16th-century castle. Fascinating, especially if you like clockwork and old gadgets. There's an endless sandy beach here as well. **www.lighthousemuseum.org.uk**

More secret places on the coast

Portsoy has a great Traditional Small Boats Festival every year in late June or early July. That's when the old harbour comes alive. Try the ice-cream shop on the main street. Further west, if you follow signs for Findlater Castle, you'll discover Sunnyside Beach – just another gem on this unspoilt coast. Close by is Pennan – home of the 'Local Hero' phone box. **www.stbf.bizland.com**

Local, Portsoy

More to explore

A winter fire festival

Stonehaven's Hogmanay (31st December) features the locals swinging fireballs as they take to the streets. Then they hurl the fireballs into the harbour.

Believe it or not

Elvis Presley's ancestors are said to come from a little community deep in the north-east farmlands, at Lonmay. Meanwhile, Walt Disney is supposed to have modelled his Disneyland logo on Craigievar Castle, near Alford.

Agricultural Shows

An annual institution in this area, agricultural shows are wildly popular with local folk. Try Huntly or Keith. Somehow, more authentic than Highland Games hereabouts – though you'll find these easily as well. (Aberdeen has a good one.)

Seabird cities

Fowlsheugh south of Stonehaven and Troup Head on the Moray Firth coast for awesome cliffs and thousands of seabirds.

Fancy a dip?

Stonehaven's unique art deco open-air heated salt water swimming pool is Olympic-sized and the largest of its kind in the UK. Moonlight dips are sometimes held during the summer season. www.stonehavenopenairpool.co.uk/

Angus & Dundee
Hidden secrets

Tay Bridge to Dundee

Dividing *neatly into three - coast, broad valley and uplands – Angus is also a bridge between north and central Scotland. Consequently, some visitors rush through, especially if on the fast A90 dual carriageway to Aberdeen – which is a pity. There is plenty to explore off the main road, especially in the Angus Glens which run deeply into the massif. The City of Dundee is forever associated with its industrial past, as well as its newspaper and publishing industry – hence the often quoted 'three Js' – jute, jam and journalism. Dundee now is a strong commercial centre with a thriving arts and cultural scene.*

The Reekie Linn

UNMISSABLE

Glen Prosen's Antarctic connection

Visit Dundee-berthed RRS Discovery, one of Scott of the Antarctic's vessels and learn the story of the ill-fated expedition. Stop by the cairn by the side of the road into Glen Prosen. Robert Falcon Scott and Dr Edward Adrian Wilson planned their famous expedition nearby. The cairn marks their favourite view. **www.rrsdiscovery.com**

House of Pitmuies in August

In high summer, this 18th-century house with its walled garden, rose garden, alpine meadow, woodland garden and riverside walk is a 'must-see'. A blaze of colour. It lies between Arbroath and Forfar. **www.pitmuies.com**

Scotland's Niagara

The Reekie Linn (meaning 'smoky waterfall' in Scots) is sometimes called Scotland's Niagara. Park by the bridge downstream, and take the short walk up. (Path can be slippery – and it's a long way down!) You can also visit Peel Farm at nearby Bridgend of Lintrathen. Enjoy afternoon tea and take home some locally produced beef and lamb. **www.peelfarm.com**

Clova or Esk – or both?

The Angus Glens have an 'out of the world' ambience. Glen Clova offers a hint of the wild uplands. At its road-end go on foot further up Glen Doll. The Glen Clova Hotel offers sanctuary. Or in Glen Esk to the east, visit The Retreat, originally a wee folk museum in a former shooting lodge, now totally refurbished. **www.gleneskretreat.btik.com**

Edzell Castle and Gardens

WORTH A LOOK

Montrose Air Station Heritage Centre

On the rabbit-cropped coastal turf north of Montrose was the UK's very first operational military airfield, set up by the Royal Flying Corps in 1913. Frequent fatal training accidents allow the enterprising museum on the site to bill itself 'the most haunted place in Britain'. Tales of phantom airmen and their planes, though manifestations not guaranteed. **www.rafmontrose.org.uk**

Edzell Castle And Garden

This is an elegant 16th century residence and was home to the Lindsays. Check out the beautiful walled garden framed by unique heraldic sculptures and carved panels; in fact the architectural framework surrounding the garden is unique in Britain. Also don't miss the tower house – a fine example of a typical 16th-century nobleman's residence. **www.historic-scotland.gov.uk**

White and Brown Caterthuns

Two separate fortified hilltops. What were they for? Defence? Ritual? They've got great views over the broad valley of Strathmore - but this is, ultimately, an ancient and unknowable spot. There is, however, a picnic site and they could be tied in with a visit to Edzell Castle. **www.historic-scotland.gov.uk**

Peter Pan Statue

The Arbroath Smokie

An Arbroath Smokie is a split and smoked haddock. (Do not confuse with a kipper, which once was a herring.) The process easily explains the prevailing and not unpleasant odour in the older fishing town of Arbroath, by the harbour. Let your nose be your guide to the nearest smoke-house. Look for the local surnames Spink and Swankie. The Arbroath Smokie stars in Arbroath's SeaFest, usually a weekend in mid August. **www.angusahead.com**

Kirriemuir and Peter Pan

This quaint red sandstone town with winding streets is the birthplace of JM Barrie, the creator of Peter Pan. His house is now a museum in the care of the National Trust for Scotland. Good local museum also in the town centre – and try the ice-cream at Visocchi's – a traditional Italian café that has been at the heart of the community for generations. **www.nts.org.uk**

Arbroath Smokies

More to explore

Lunan Bay

Big sandy beach, easy parking. The ruinous Red Castle is your landmark. Between Arbroath and Montrose. Look for agates on the shore. Or, at least, pretty wave-polished pebbles.

Forfar – Home of the bridie

Folded-over pastry holds a filling of chopped meat and onions. Substantial fayre, associated with this market town. Try McLaren & Son, bakers in the town.

A Lot About Jute

Verdant Works is a real find of a museum – remembering, celebrating and explaining Dundee's jute industry – just west of the city centre.

www.rrsdiscovery.com

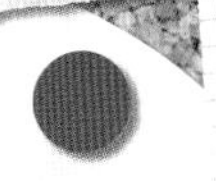

Pick Your Own

Family run Broadslap Fruit Farm cater for most berry needs; strawberries, raspberries, gooseberries, blackcurrants and redcurrants. Just off the A9 at Broom of Dalreoch, south west of Perth.

While Sensational, the Dundee Science Centre, is a hands-on fun place for youngsters, it is also the only place in Scotland where you can try Mindball. Two people sit with electrodes strapped to their heads. The one who is the calmest is able to move the ball – using only their thoughts – down the table and score a goal. Just a trifle unsettling...

www.sensation.org.uk

Perthshire

Hidden secrets

RIVER BRAAN

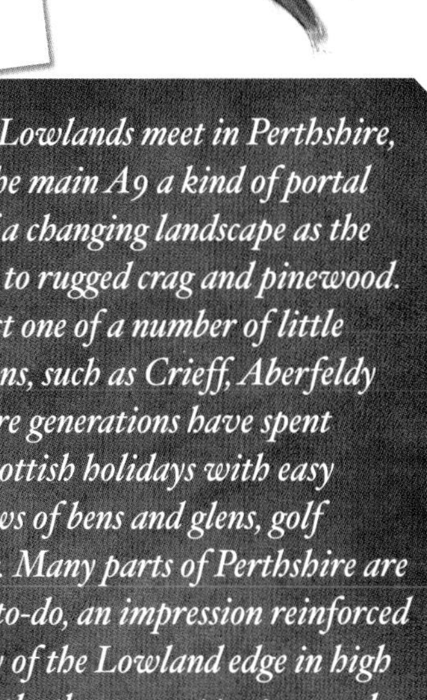

HIGHLANDS and Lowlands meet in Perthshire, with Dunkeld by the main A9 a kind of portal with a real sense of a changing landscape as the soft fields give way to rugged crag and pinewood. And Dunkeld is just one of a number of little Highland-edge towns, such as Crieff, Aberfeldy and Pitlochry, where generations have spent their traditional Scottish holidays with easy access to bonny views of bens and glens, golf courses and angling. Many parts of Perthshire are unashamedly well-to-do, an impression reinforced by the rich greenery of the Lowland edge in high summer. Consequently, the area supports a good number of quality shops and restaurants, some in surprisingly rural locations. In contrast, above the Highland line, it is easy to find solitude and high wild places. In short, Perthshire has a lot to offer.

Rannoch Moor

UNMISSABLE

Knock Hill Delights

Stroll up the Knock Hill, above the hilly little resort town of Crieff. It takes a bit of time but the reward is out of proportion to the effort. For sheer variety of landscape on the very edge of the Highlands, probably one of Scotland's finest views.

A Rannoch Moor Picnic

Buy provisions in Aberfeldy (butcher has deli counter). Drive to road end beyond Loch Rannoch. Consume picnic and impress your companion by reading RL Stevenson's adventure story 'Kidnapped', which was inspired by the local surroundings. Atmospheric? Nowhere else quite like it…

Killiecrankie

If given the choice between a Highland broadsword or jumping 18½ft (5.5m) across rocks with a rushing river below, you'd probably go for the jump, wouldn't you? Judge for yourself at the Soldier's Leap, by the 1689 Jacobite battlesite at Killiecrankie, north of Pitlochry. Discover riverside walks through the oakwoods, close to the A9. A good autumn excursion. A visitor centre tells the story. **www.nts.org.uk**

Enchanted Forest

WORTH A LOOK

Touring the Perthshire loops

Discover a rural byway through Glen Quaich, crossing high-level moorland with delectable mountain views. (A notice says that the road will not be cleared if it snows – so check the weather forecast first.) Heading north-west, the route drops by a spectacular series of hairpin bends down to Kenmore. There are shops and a hotel here including the Courtyard Restaurant, Brasserie and Bar, where the open fire can be very welcoming.

A Real Enchanted Forest

For young and old, the Enchanted Forest in Faskally Woods, near Pitlochry, is a light and sound experience like no other. Different theme every year and runs in Oct/Nov – buses from the centre of Pitlochry. **www.enchantedforest.org.uk**

All's fair in Aberfeldy

Discover a very pleasing and well resourced little Scottish town in the hills – especially when it comes to wild and wet adventures like white river rafting and safaris. It has a distillery and nearby gardens to visit, a good selection of places to eat, and, best of all, a selection of little shops to browse around. It is also Scotland's first Fairtrade town. And the town's bread is baked by a local artisan baker at the Breadalbane Bakery.

Branklyn Garden

WORTH A LOOK *(continued)*

Comrie and the Devil

Don't hurry through Comrie without checking out the gallery, deli, baker and other shops along its main street. Then explore Glen Lednock, a lovely little glen behind the town, a sometimes overlooked location. You'll find a signpost to the De'il's Cauldron – an impressive waterfall. It's tree-shady, deep and lively but with strong wooden walkways and handrails provided, you'll be fine! Good walking hereabouts, too.

Gardens to visit

Branklyn Garden in Perth is well worth tracking down. Go there in late spring when the peat-loving blue poppies, the famous Meconopsis are in bloom. It's small (only two acres) and hence intimate and shady. It's completely different from the formality of Drummond Castle Gardens, south of Crieff. If the garden looks a little familiar, it was a movie location in Rob Roy starring Liam Neeson.

www.nts.org.uk | www.drummondcastlegardens.co.uk

Perth and Cittaslow

Perth has become Scotland's first Cittaslow town. From environmental awareness to promoting local food initiatives, the Cittaslow movement is all about good food, local produce and traditional production methods. That means, in practical terms, a good selection of places to eat at every level, plus food events such as the Perth Farmer's Market, on the first Saturday of every month.

www.pkc.gov.uk

More to explore

Big Tree Country

The Hermitage at Dunkeld has one of Britain's tallest trees, a Douglas Fir, at c. 212ft (64.5m). Britain's tallest hedge, an extraordinary 100ft (30m) high beech, is at Meikleour near Blairgowrie.
www.perthshirebigtreecountry.co.uk

The mighty River Tay

At 120 miles, it's the longest in Scotland, and the largest, carrying more water than the Thames and Severn combined. Largest ever salmon caught in Scotland was from the Tay, caught by a lady angler in 1922. It weighed 64 lbs. (29kgs).

Blairgowrie and Soft Fruit

Around Blairgowrie and over into Angus is the largest fruit-growing area in the EU. Along with other local flavours, some soft fruits find their way into the delightfully eccentric Scottish fruit wine-maker Cairn O'Mohr's products. Visit them off the A90 near Errol, between Perth and Dundee.
www.cairnomohr.co.uk

Traditional Sweeties

The town of Crieff has quite a few traditional shops. Gordon and Durward make their own sweets in flavours you may remember from your childhood. It's certainly a colourful window display.
www.scottishsweets.co.uk

Beatrix Potter and that Rabbit

Holidaying in Dunkeld in 1893, Beatrix Potter started to write about a certain naughty bunny to a friend. The character became Peter Rabbit. Find out more at the Beatrix Potter Garden and Exhibition at Birnam.

Argyll, the Isles Loch Lomond, Stirling and Trossachs

Hidden secrets

IONA, INNER HEBRIDES

…ght uncertainty they lie,
…e future joys to Fancy's eye.

THIS *is where tourism began. The Romantic poets (like Wordsworth) composed their verse in praise of the Trossachs, even before Sir Walter Scott put the area on the map. Later, the Clyde became the great escape for the 'Second City of the Empire' as Glasgow went 'doon the watter' for a short summer break, perhaps to Rothesay and Dunoon. Towns like Oban with their rail and ferry connections have been traditional holiday destinations for generations. With mossy woods around the long fingers of sea-lochs, its soft air and distant sea views, the call of the west is strong. It's a beguiling sort of place, with its salty, tangy essence captured for some in a peaty malt whisky.*

Isle of Colonsay

UNMISSABLE

Duncan Ban McIntyre Monument, Dalmally

Unmissable, yet often missed, and signposted from Dalmally village. Old road to Inveraray driveable as far as Monument. Superb vista over Loch Awe and Ben Cruachan from this 19th-century rotunda. McIntyre was a Gaelic poet sometimes described as 'the Robert Burns of the Highlands'.

The island of Colonsay

A Hebridean jewel. Varied landscapes for such a small island, not just wildlife but also a very natural golf course. (Rabbits and sheep hazards.) Environmentally speaking, consider not taking a car. Most of the island is walkable – but if visiting neighbouring little island Oransay (to see ancient priory) check tide times, as beach linking the two islands disappears at high tide.

How to see the Corryvreckan Whirlpool

Ferry to Islay, ferry to Jura, drive to the end of the motorable section of the only road, then walk. Alternatively, a number of boat operators in the Oban area will take you to see this spectacular area of turbulence off the north end of Jura. (Just don't go in a gale – there are standing waves 15ft high under these conditions!) **www.seafari.co.uk**

Endrick Cascades

WORTH A LOOK

The Endrick Cascades

Not signposted, this 90ft waterfall on the River Endrick is close to the main B818, west of the Carron Valley reservoir. Good picnic spot, mostly known by the locals. Westbound, look for stile by left side of the road after bridge over the Endrick Water.

The Paradise Pools by Sheriffmuir

Out of the way yet close to Scotland's central belt. Northbound from Stirling, left after the Wallace Monument (just before large roundabout). Note carpark for popular Dumyat walk but continue till Black Hill is on the right. Pools and waterfalls nearby. (See OS map 57. Sheriffmuir Inn is also nearby. Great for summer evening drinks outside.)

Callander Crags and the Bracklinn Falls

Above the busy town of Callander, the Crags are easily found at the far end of the town (coming in from south). Follow the line of crags eastwards, dropping down to Bracklinn Falls carpark and return to town. Just the place to try out your new boots and outdoor gear – good choice of shops on Callander main street.

Glen Finglas

A side glen off the main Trossachs circular drive, peaceful Glen Finglas is where the Pre-Raphaelite artist Millais fell in love with Effie, the wife of crusty critic, Ruskin. Glen worth a walk, with The Byre Inn and the old institution of the Brig o' Turk Tea Room, both by the main road at Brig o' Turk.

Loch Katrine

Loch Katrine - where Wordsworth got it wrong

Most visitors only go to Loch Katrine's east end. Discover Rob Roy country at the other end of the loch. Walk west from Stronachlachar Pier, round the head of the loch, past Glen Gyle house (Rob's birthplace). Beyond Portnellan (where Rob once lived) is a poignant Macgregor graveyard. Wordsworth also came here, writing a poem called 'Rob Roy's Grave'. Er...actually it's in Balquhidder.

St Blane's Chapel, Bute

On this traditional holiday island, most head for the beaches. Instead, wander around St Blane's Chapel, right at the south end – it's peaceful and timeless beneath the trees – and there's a signposted walk to the coast nearby. Back in Rothesay enjoy coffee at Musicker (opposite castle), a café that sells guitars. (Or is it a guitar shop that does nice cakes and paninis?) **www.musicker.co.uk**

Iona Beaches

This is a very popular excursion. Most visit the restored abbey and the historic surroundings of the burial place of ancient Scottish kings. But make sure you allow time to head across the island to discover the little white beaches of the west side. Easily walkable – best to climb the little (and curiously named) hill Dun I to spy out your route in advance.

More to explore

Hollytree Hotel
Once a railway station on a long-vanished branch line. Superb views across Loch Linnhe to Ardgour Hills. Local boat supplies their seafood. Squat lobsters to die for.
www.hollytyreehotel.co.uk

View up Loch Lomond
Park in Drymen and nip into the little garden area (through the gate) opposite the Buchanan Arms. Fine panorama of the loch instantly opens up looking northwards.

View down Loch Lomond
Park near Inverarnan at the north end of the loch and walk south along the West Highland Way until a brilliant southward view appears by the deserted hamlet of Blairstainge.

Afloat on Loch Lomond
Best way to discover Loch Lomond islands. Take a mail boat cruise from Balmaha or hire your own rowing boat. Macfarlane and Sons have contract to deliver mail. Check in advance.
www.balmahaboatyard.co.uk/mailboat.html

Coast Restaurant, Oban
Peace and tranquillity moments from the main street bustle. Modern Scottish cuisine.
www.coastoban.com

THE WHANGIE

STRANGE ROCK FORMATION BETWEEN BEARSDEN AND DRYMEN, OFF A809. NICE EVENING EXCURSION. YET ANOTHER LOCH LOMOND VIEWPOINT.

ABERFOYLE INTERNATIONAL MUSHROOM FESTIVAL WEEKEND IN OCTOBER. CELEBRATE SCOTLAND'S VARIETY FROM CHANTERELLE TO PORCINI...

KILCHURN CASTLE

ROMANTIC RUIN ON THE EDGE OF LOCH AWE ACCESSED ON FOOT FROM MAIN ROAD. AT WEST END OF LOCH (TAKE CARE ON LEVEL CROSSING.)

WWW.VISITSCOTLAND.COM/WALKING

FERRY GATEWAYS TO ARGYLL

IF HEADING FOR KNAPDALE OR KINTYRE, CONSIDER SHORTENING THE DRIVE BY GOING GOUROCK TO DUNOON (23 MIN CROSSING), THEN CROSSING COWAL TO REACH PORTAVADIE. FERRY CONNECTION THERE TO TARBERT TAKES 25 MINS.

WWW.CALMAC.CO.UK

The Kingdom of Fife

Hidden secrets

CRAIL HARBOUR

FIFE is frequently referred to as a kingdom. That's a reminder that it's a place with plenty of character. In ancient days this land between two firths really was a kingdom – an independently ruled Pictish state. Today, the west of Fife and its industrial heritage includes such gems as Culross. The east, historically untouched by the Industrial Revolution, offers not just sparkling sea views south across the Firth of Forth from the 'East Neuk' (Scots: corner) villages, but also a reputation as an area for some of Scotland's finest golf. It's all very neat and well tended, in the east, with red-roofed villages, lush hedgerows and ripening barley fields – classic lowland Scotland.

Culross Palace

UNMISSABLE

A period-piece at Crail

Crail is one of the most photogenic of all the East Neuk of Fife villages. Crail's 16th-century Tolbooth, with its Dutch-cast bell of 1520, overlooks the old market place and the setting still seems to echo of long-vanished burgh market days. Down at the tiny harbour is a hut where you can order your cooked lobster, if the boats have been out.

Hidden Falkland

Falkland, with its red roofs and imposing palace in the centre, is one of the prettiest villages in Fife. But don't overlook the walks on the Falkland Estate at the other end of the village. These are a good way of exploring the soft green countryside of the old kingdom. **www.centreforstewardship.org.uk**.

Siege warfare in St Andrews

Ruined St Andrews Castle occupies a headland overlooking the sea and offers one very unusual experience. Follow a 16th-century 'countermine' – a tunnel dug out from the castle by its defenders to thwart besieging forces trying to tunnel their way in! It's all vivid history (though you'll probably still be happy to re-emerge above ground!) **www.historic-scotland.gov.uk**

A time capsule in Culross

Culross once lead the way in coal mining and salt pans, but was bypassed by the Industrial Revolution. Many 17th and 18th-century domestic buildings survived. Now restored, the older part has the air of a film set. Visit the Palace, the townhouse of Sir George Bruce, a 16th century local entrepreneur. **www.nts.org.uk**

St Andrews Castle

WORTH A LOOK

Meet the past in St Andrews

The ordinary lives and affairs of generations of St Andrews folk are recalled in the St Andrews Preservation Trust Museum. It's got a secluded restored garden adjacent. Housed in a 17th-century house in the fishers' quarter of the town by the harbour, this is a good place to pause and take a break from sight-seeing.
www.sapt.demon.co.uk

An energy-saving saint at Pittenweem

Pittenweem's white-harled, crow-stepped gabled houses cluster round its busy harbour. The name Pittenweem is from an old Gaelic word 'uamh' meaning cave. The shrine of St Fillan, in a cave, still survives here, up a close (alleyway) that leads from the harbour. They say this saint was able to write by night as he had a luminous arm.

The harbourmaster at Dysart

The coastal community of Dysart has had a colourful past as a trading port. Today, the Harbourmaster's House is restored and displays the historic background and encourages you to explore the area, especially by way of the Fife Coastal Path. This runs all the way round Fife for 150km [94 miles].
www.theharbourmastershouse.co.uk

A famous philanthropist

Carnegie gave away $350 million. At the Andrew Carnegie Birthplace Museum in Dunfermline, they'll tell you he was one of the first people in the USA able to understand morse code 'down the wire' just by listening (as opposed to writing it down first). This enabled him to get and act on information ahead of his competitors. **www.carnegiebirthplace.com**

Scottish landscapes in Kirkcaldy

At the Kirkcaldy Museum and Art Gallery, see the largest public collection outside the National Galleries of Scotland of the works of William McTaggart and Scottish Colourist S.J. Peploe. The collection also includes a significant number of works by the Glasgow Boys. Museum section has Wemyss Ware pottery, the characteristic and colourful local ceramic ware formerly produced in the town. **www.fifedirect.org.uk**

Wemyss Caves

In the sandstone rock by the shore between East and West Wemyss, this series of ancient caves have had a troubled history over the years, with mining, war, vandalism, and sea-storm all damaging their precious contents: drawings from Pictish times, including what is thought to be the earliest boat representation in Scotland. (Channel 4's Time Team investigated this site in 2005.) **www.wemysscaves.co.uk**

A mansion in the countryside

Discover Hill of Tarvit House, a fine Edwardian mansion with interesting collections of furniture and paintings, and an attractive garden, plus a 40 acre estate. Hire a picnic hamper from the National Trust for Scotland who look after the place, and choose a selection from their tea room to fill it. Pick up an estate map and you'll soon find a picnic spot. **www.nts.org.uk**

More to explore

AWARD-WINNING FISH AND CHIPS AT ANSTRUTHER. BEST TO VISIT OFF-PEAK, TO AVOID QUEUES. SIT IN OR TAKE AWAY. WWW.ANSTRUTHERFISHBAR.CO.UK

NOT JUST THE OLD COURSE THERE IS MILE UPON MILE OF LINKS COURSES UP THIS COAST, SOME REAL HIDDEN GEMS INCLUDING OPEN QUALIFIERS – WWW.VISITSCOTLAND.COM/GOLF

CAIRNIE FRUIT FARM NEAR CUPAR, HAVE PICK-YOUR-OWN, AND THEY DO CREAM TEAS AND STRAWBERRY TEAS IN SEASON. WWW.CAIRNIEFRUITFARM.CO.UK

CAMBO ESTATE NEAR ST ANDREWS MAKES AN INTERESTING VISIT AT ANY TIME OF YEAR. IN THE SNOWDROP SEASON, THERE ARE OVER 200 VARIETIES OF THEM HERE! WWW.CAMBOSNOWDROPS.COM

EARTHSHIP FIFE VISITOR CENTRE IS SCOTLAND'S FIRST EARTHSHIP. IT'S A SELF-SUSTAINING ECOLOGICAL DEVELOPMENT WITH A VISITOR CENTRE. WWW.SCI-SCOTLAND.ORG.UK

SCOTLAND'S SECRET BUNKER IS AN ABANDONED GOVERNMENT COMMAND AND CONTROL CENTRE – LEGACY OF THE COLD WAR! IT'S OPEN TO VISITORS BUT CAN'T SAY WHERE IT IS EXACTLY – IT'S A SECRET. (ACTUALLY, IT'S NORTH OF ANSTRUTHER.) WWW.SECRETBUNKER.CO.UK

Edinburgh & the Lothians

Hidden secrets

The Royal Mile & Edinburgh Castle

Edinburgh - *'The Athens of the North' – doesn't just depend on its wealth of elegant neoclassical architecture for its status. The sheer theatricality of castle and crag, romantic spires of the Old Town and so on, form a backdrop to Edinburgh as a cultural centre with an international reputation. After all, it's the setting for the world's largest arts and culture festival every August. But if you need some quiet time from the city bustle, then the Lothians lie in an arc around the city. Here, you can enjoy plenty of unspoilt open spaces: for example, country parks in West Lothian, city panoramas from the broad grassy ridges of the Pentland Hills, and beautiful sandy beaches stretching out to the east.*

Dean Village

UNMISSABLE

A (Sheep's) Heid for heights

From the foot of the Royal Mile, step out through the park for Edinburgh's oldest pub. The Sheep Heid Inn is in Duddingston village, round the back of Arthur's Seat. Down by the nearby loch there's a secret garden – Dr Neil's Garden, open in summer – where it's hard to believe you're so close to the city centre. **www.sheepheid.co.uk**

Village in the city

Dean Village is a ten minute walk from Princes Street. Follow Queensferry Street to the Dean Bridge. Look for Bell's Brae adjacent and follow it downhill. Walks along the river in both directions. Downstream is the neo-classical St Bernard's Well. You emerge in Stockbridge. Nice little shops here – and the Botanics are only a little further. **www.deanvillage.org**

Pentland Hill views

Wild country close to the city? By bus or car, look for layby (right) on straight on A702, running south-west by the Pentland Hills, about two miles beyond Flotterstone. Signpost says Balerno, over the hills. Follow path to heathery coll, then it's another sharp pull (right again) to top of Carnethy Hill. Panorama southwards to Lammermuirs especially good. **www.visitmidlothian.com**

PENTLAND HILLS

WORTH A LOOK

A MANSION...

You've done the castle, the palace and strolled around the National Galleries. Time to look further afield? Check out Lauriston Castle at the west side of the city, three miles from Princes Street. Set in 30 acres of parkland and formal gardens, it's a 19th-century mansion built round a 16th-century tower. Interesting interiors and furniture. **www.cac.org.uk/venues/lauriston.htm**

A GARDEN...

Malleny Garden is at Balerno and this three acre walled garden set in nine acres of woodland and policies is a peaceful haven where you can sit quietly and plan your next foray. **www.nts.org.uk**

A SHOP OR TWO

Bruntsfield, Churchhill, Morningside – not quite village Edinburgh but certainly where real Edinburgh life goes on aside from the main tourist places. A well-to-do area with good shopping and nice cafés. Café Grande just one place with a loyal following. **www.cafegrande.co.uk**

CAFE GRANDE

Linlithgow Loch and Palace

WORTH A LOOK *(continued)*

Lunch at Linlithgow?

Old established Linlithgow is noted for Linlithgow Palace – where the Stuart monarchs of Scotland held court. Lovers of a fine lunch will afterwards head for Michelin-starred Champany Inn, north-east over the M9, where local beef is treated with rare (or medium) reverence. The Chop and Ale House is less formal than the main restaurant, and booking is not required. **www.champany.com**

A discovery - the East Lothian coastline

A wholesome pub lunch at The Prestoungrange Gothenburg, a kind of cooperative pub at Prestonpans, then down the coast via Aberlady Bay (birdy) and Gullane (golfy). Dirleton features ancient Dirleton Castle or park at Yellowcraigs to enjoy the beach. The Scottish Seabird Centre at North Berwick is the 5-star place for birdwatching. Take tea on the terrace, perhaps. **www.seabird.org**

Eat local

Worth checking out Dunbar based Knowes Farm shop if you're down the East Lothian coast. East Lothian Food and Drink Festival takes place every year promoting the geat array of natural produce available in this area. **www.foodanddrinkeastlothian.com**

More to explore

Where to eat near Haymarket Station? First Coast comes recommended as a quality neighbourhood bistro. Scottish specialities include 'spoots' (razorclams).
www.first-coast.co.uk

Arniston House

A Georgian mansion to visit just outside Edinburgh, a wonderful (inhabited) building designed by William Adam.
www.arniston-house.co.uk

The Edinburgh Pass

Package includes entry to 30 top attractions plus transport around the city. Check it out at www.edinburghpass.com

Linlithgow Book Festival

Open mike readings, workshops and lots more literary; runs October/November.
www.linlithgowbookfestival.org

Scottish Poetry Library

Wonderful words to enjoy in a deliberatively restful setting, with oak cladding and blue-glazed terracotta tiles. More architectural cleverness fitting modernity into an Old Town close.
www.spl.org.uk

Glasgow & the Clyde Valley

Hidden secrets

Royal Exchange Square

Glasgow, *Scotland's largest city, offers upbeat 'café society' and nightlife. It is simply the best shopping experience in the UK outside London – thanks mostly to 'the Golden Z', the shape of Sauchiehall Street, Buchanan Street and Argyle Street. 'Glasgow style' is also linked to architecture and the city's association with Charles Rennie Mackintosh. Another part of its distinctive culture and identity is the city's reputation for friendliness – an endearing feature you'll notice in pubs, shops and restaurants. Finally, locals will readily tell you that Glasgow translates as 'dear green place' – they say there are more than 70 parks and formal gardens within its boundaries.*

The Lighthouse

UNMISSABLE

The Lighthouse – Scotland's centre for architecture and design

Not a lighthouse at all, but a modification of a former newspaper office, designed by the architectural firm where Mackintosh was an apprentice. Highlight is the city views from the Mackintosh Tower and also from the top floor viewing platform. **www.thelighthouse.co.uk**

The Merchant City

A reference to the old 'tobacco lords' – the 18th century entrepreneurs trading with the Americas – the Merchant City, east of Buchanan Street is a happening place, with its quirky and designer shops, award winning restaurants and vibrant bars. Babbity Bowster is a long established favourite watering hole and meeting place – listen to the local banter. **www.merchantcityfestival.com**

Glasgow Necropolis

The Victorians certainly departed in style. This 'garden cemetery' by the medieval Glasgow Cathedral offers great city views as well as monuments to the wealthy and prominent citizens which were designed by leading Glasgow architects such as Alexander 'Greek' Thomson and (inevitably), Charles Rennie Macintosh. **www.glasgownecropolis.org**

The Falls of Clyde

New Lanark is famed as a World Heritage Site. This Utopian experiment in workers welfare is fascinating – but make sure you allow time for a stroll upstream, away from the village, to see the 'linns' (Scots: waterfalls), especially Corra Linn (90ft). Follow waymarked paths. (Scottish Wildlife Trust reserve. They advise to look out for badger 'snuffle holes'. And why not?) **www.newlanark.org**

Ashton Lane

WORTH A LOOK

West End

Shopping and entertainment isn't all in the Buchanan Street and Merchant City areas. Byres Road is well worth a stroll, with Ashton Lane running parallel. Bars and restaurants in plenty. If you like your tea, try Tchai-Ovna, a tea shop on Otago Lane serving over 80 kinds from all over the world.

Greenbank Gardens, Clarkston

Ornamental walled garden, subdivided and designed to inspire small-scale domestic gardeners. Also features National Collection of Bergenia (in Scots: 'elephant's lugs'). On the way, stop off in the swish Eat Deli on Busby Road for picnic supplies; homemade salads recommended. **www.nts.org.uk**

Parnie Street

Behind Trongate – so not as genteel, perhaps, as the West End - you'll find in Parnie Street rows of brightly coloured shops selling old comics, vintage clothes, model cars etc. Bars, the Tron Theatre and art galleries as well in this down-to-earth area.

John St, Merchant City

More in the West End

Thistle Books and Voltaire & Rousseau: second-hand book shops, both off Otago Street. Thistle Books share premises with a vintage sheet-music store. Voltaire & Rousseau is an Aladdin's cave of a place, stuffed with books of varying age and quality; occasionally in alphabetical order, although that's probably just a coincidence.

The Victorian Village

Over three floors in West Regent Street, a cornucopia of vintage jewellery, accessories, clothes, lace and antique furniture, ceramics and ornaments.

Lochwinnoch – RSPB Reserve

One of the few wetlands in the west of Scotland, stop off at Lochwinnoch en route for the Clyde coast perhaps. There's a pleasing, peaceful reeds-and-lapping-water air about this place. Combine with lunch at the Brown Bull, family-run, real ale village pub. **www.rspb.org.uk**

Falls of Clyde

More to explore

Stravaigin: West End

Restaurant (Gibson Street) with a reputation for menus built from diverse world influences while focusing on the best of Scottish ingredients.

Fifi & Ally

Fashion and lifestyle store high up in the retail temple that is Princes Square. Features café/patisserie called the Cupping Salon, with exclusive designer creations – a place to see and be seen.

www.fifi-and-ally.com

Out of town

View Loch Lomond's islands by going up the east side of Loch Lomond to Balmaha, then climbing Conic Hill. (It's on the West Highland Way) Great panorama, right on the Highland edge.

Glengoyne Distillery

Good choice for a distillery visit without travelling too far. About 15 miles north of Glasgow, it offers the most in depth range of tours, one of which allows you to create your own blended whisky.

www.glengoyne.com

Brazen

Voted most stylish boutique 2007 at the Scottish Style Awards; cutting edge jewellery and accessories, worth a browse for the décor alone. Find it in Albion Street, Merchant City.

www.brazenstudios.co.uk

Britannica Panopticon Music Hall, Trongate

A music hall built in 1857, last of its type in Scotland - once the main place of entertainment for locals. Stan Laurel, Cary Grant and others like them have had turns there; closed in 1938 and lay empty but intact until recently. For shows and occasional tours, keep an eye on - www.glasgowmerchantcity.net/britanniapanopticontrust.htm

A Play, a Pie and a Pint

Oran Mor (corner of Great Western Road and Byres Road] have lunchtime performances - perfect way to while away a couple of hours and get fed and watered at the same time. www.oran-mor.co.uk/playpiepint

The Clockwork Beer Company

Hidden in the Southside near Hampden Stadium, beside the railway bridge, this pub has its own microbrewery on site serving their own beer plus countless others. Easily recognised by a giant key that is part of the name on the façade. But avoid on Scotland match days where you might be refused entry without a ticket, a kilt and face paint!!

Ayrshire & Arran

Hidden secrets

The New Bridge, Ayr

Look *from the train as it travels coast-wise in Ayrshire and you'd be forgiven for thinking that it's one continuous golf course. It's a reminder that the Clyde coast in Ayrshire is associated with recreation – and golf in particular. Rural Ayrshire means lush fields and clipped hawthorn hedges, wooded river valleys and hills. Your eye is drawn to the unmistakable outline of Arran, often referred to as 'The Sleeping Warrior'. This island has been a traditional holiday playground for generations. And one more thing: you can't travel in this area without encountering a certain farmer, pausing behind his horse drawn plough and crooning over some old Scots song while struggling with a rhyme. It's Robert Burns – and he's everywhere!*

Brodick Castle

UNMISSABLE

Brodick Castle and its rhododendrons

All the acquisitions and sporting trophies of the Dukes of Hamilton can be viewed indoors here. Outside there are nationally important collections of rhododendrons. You can sound knowledgeable by remarking that you can't beat the old Azalea luteum for scent. (It's the deciduous bright yellow one). If you do sit outdoors at the café here, beware the especially bold chaffinches. **www.nts.org.uk**

Machrie Moor Stone Circles

Great views to Arran's mountains from this atmospheric place on the west side of the island, with its complex of standing stones and other hints of prehistoric settlement. Like other ancient places it asks the question: what was going on here? Allow a couple of hours.

Machrie Moor Stone Circles

Burns House Museum Exhibit

WORTH A LOOK

Burns' little town

East of Ayr, and sometimes overlooked as so many visitors go to Alloway, is the little town of Mauchline, sitting on a ridge above the agricultural land. There is a cluster of Burns-linked places here, including the Burns House Museum and there is a view of the Burns Memorial Tower at the edge of town.

The Electric Brae

What's this all about? The A719 south of Ayr, near Culzean Castle. Down looks like up and vice-versa – so that cars appear to roll uphill. Weird. And it's got nothing to do with electricity. It's an optical illusion caused by the local topography.

Village of Dunure

A good place to dip into the breezy ambience of the Clyde coast. Historic harbour and picturesque ruined castle on nearby headland makes a worthwhile stroll. Check for fresh seafood – local langoustines, lobster etc - on offer at the Dunure Inn. Agates sometimes found on pebbly beach.

Burns House Museum

Lochranza Castle

Tibbie's Brig

Local poetess, friend of Robert Burns (and illegal whisky distiller) recalled in restored bridge. Down a track off road to Kames, south of Muirkirk, A70. Good place to sample ambience of upland Ayrshire. By the River Ayr Way walking route. Good picnic place: look for Kingfishers on river. **www.ayrshirepaths.org.uk**

Lochranza

Picturesque castle, distillery visitor centre and pleasant setting make this an Arran 'must see'. Also spectacular spiky view of the Arran hills on road from here to Corrie. Stroll coast-wise north from Lochranza to see 'Hutton's Unconformity' – famous geological feature first noted by James Hutton in 1786. Crucial in shaping theories of the age of our planet.

The King's Cave

The actual place on Arran where King Robert I (the Bruce), dispirited and defeated, was inspired to 'try, try again' after watching a web-building spider. Actually, probably not. It's an invention of Sir Water Scott. No matter – still a fine coastal walk, accessible from north, south or the main road through Forestry Commission planting at Torr Righ Mor, south of Machrie.

More to explore

Silver Sands at Kildonan, Arran

Lovely spot – down steps off road east of Kildonan.

Burns Country Smokehouse, Minishant

Highest quality smoked products produced in artisan fashion using raw materials from 'Freedom Food' sources. They smoke their salmon using staves from old malt whisky barrels. Also farm shop and coffee shop.

Taste of Arran

The little shop by the creamery in Brodick Castle's former home farm sells the locally made product – just one of several food producers on the island. (Try the ice cream as well.)

www.taste-of-arran.co.uk

Burns landmarks in Alloway

It's the done thing to visit the Burns features – Cottage, Alloway Auld Kirk, Monument etc – but remember that there are also guided walks to further interpret the area. Check with Ayr visitor information centre.

Cleats Shore, Arran

At the south end of the island, this is, apparently, the only official nudist beach in Scotland.

Dumfries & Galloway

Hidden secrets

Sweetheart Abbey

Sometimes *overlooked by visitors travelling too intently north, the south-western part of Scotland has plenty of character. The backdrop of lonely hills roll down to pasture and extensive woods and these, in turn, give way to rich farmlands and a sunny south facing coast. The palm trees thriving at Logan Botanic Gardens are proof of a mild climate - lots of gardens to visit - and there are castles and photogenic villages to reach by quiet rural roads. In short, Galloway does the picturesque very well – in fact, the colourful frontages of the little towns, such as Kirkcudbright, are enough to inspire you to pack that box of water colour paints, just in case!*

Loch Trool

UNMISSABLE

Galloway Forest Park and stunning Loch Trool

Galloway is rugged, natural and unspoiled. Drive through picturesque Glentrool Village to the Loch car parks where you can see the commemorative stone recalling Robert the Bruce's battle here. No need to stroll far for a sense of the grandeur of the place – unless the fit-looking walkers make you feel guilty – they're on their way up The Merrick, highest hill in the South of Scotland.

Caerlaverock when it's cold

Caerlaverock Castle is fascinating but tie in your visit here with some wide-open Solway spaces. Near the castle are large areas of marsh, foreshore and field accessible via the Wildlfowl and Wetlands Trust Centre at Eastpark Farm. Deluxe heated hides – just the job for a winter visit! Barnacle geese are the speciality here – flypasts are spectacular. **www.historic-scotland.gov.uk**

Caerlaverlock Castle

LOGAN BOTANIC GARDENS

Castle Kennedy Gardens

Most of us manage with a barrow, but the Earl of Stair who created the original Castle Kennedy Gardens used a squad of troops for the main landscape features. All is on a grand scale – vistas down monkey puzzle avenues, thickets of rhododendrons, vistas across lakes. Thank goodness for a nice cup of tea and home bakes at the gardens' tearoom!
www.castlekennedygardens.co.uk

The Almorness peninsula

By woods and rough pasture, with coastal views on every side, this is an excellent but little-known walk out and into the bay. Horse Isles Bay and White Port beaches are worth discovering and treats you to wide views of the Solway out towards Heston Island. Check tide times if intending further coastal exploring.

CASTLE KENNEDY GARDENS

THE GREY MARE'S TAIL

WORTH A LOOK

THE GREY MARE'S TAIL WATERFALL AND MOFFAT

Remember your school geography lesson about hanging valleys? This one is a classic – the waterfall tumbles 200ft off the lip of the upper valley. Its source is Loch Skene and it's a revelation if you make the climb: wild country and lonely hills. Another reminder the south of Scotland can be quite wild. After your walk head back into the charming historic market town of Moffat to buy your supply of Moffat Toffee. **www.nts.org.uk**

ROCKCLIFFE TO KIPPFORD

Another view of this 'riviera coast' (at least when the tide is in). Pleasant path (NTS) links these two little communities, where the emphasis is very much on leisure and relaxing. Enjoy a drink outside, watch the yachting activity. **www.nts.org.uk**

CAVE AT WHITHORN

A must for fans of 'The Wicker Man'. Ironically, the immediate area around this cave, associated with early Christianity, featured in the cult movie. Pleasant excursions, down a leafy lane to the pebbly shore. (Note the sloe bushes on your way down the lane). **www.thewickermanfestival.co.uk**

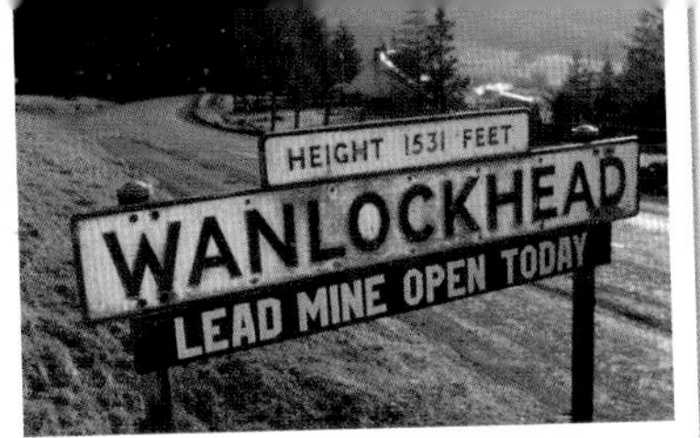

Welcome to Wanlockhead

Raiders Road

Cover the vast grounds on a forest drive on the Raiders' Road (toll charged) to out-of-the-way spots of inland Galloway. Take some time to enjoy Clatteringshaws Loch. The Otter's Pool is popular with families – or find a picnic spot by the Stroan Loch, further east, a good viewpoint here is the disused viaduct, a poignant relic of the railway age.

Gold Panning at Wanlockhead

Take the dramatic road through the Mennock Pass to reach the highest village in Scotland, Wanlockhead (1,531ft). Here at the Museum of Lead Mining you can rent or buy gold panning equipment and try it out at the museum or, with a licence, in the local river! Experience the museum's tour including the chance to go down the actual lead mine! **www.leadminingmuseum.co.uk**

Mull of Galloway

The southernmost point of Scotland. Cliff scenery. Birds galore (RSPB reserve). See Ireland, the Isle of Man, Wales and the Lake District coast on a clear day – and best of all, see them from the high headland with a fine coffee at hand from the award-winning clifftop Gallie Craig Coffee House and Tea Room. **www.galliecraig.co.uk**

More to explore

Two for One offers

Local 'See and Do' guide has a range of two for one admissions at local attractions. Check it out at a visitor information centre or request a copy online.

Ring the bell at Threave

The tower of Threave Castle is on an island on the River Dee. You have to ring a bell to summon the boatman to take you across. (Romantic or what?)

www.historic-scotland.gov.uk

Buccleuch Arms, Moffat

Outstanding service here. Try the steak pie or a hand made Buccleuch Burger at lunchtime. They use the famous Buccleuch Beef from Buccleuch Estates, as do a number of other local restaurants.

www.eatscotland.com

Bluebells in spring

Carstramon Wood is an ancient oakwood near Gatehouse-of-Fleet. Great place to see native bluebells in May.

www.wildlifetrust.org.uk

Solway salmon & sea trout

Locally caught fish available in summer. Some landed using traditional 'haaf netting' – the net design dates back to Viking times. Local places to eat wild caught fish include Somerton House Hotel, Lockerbie and Cally Palace Hotel, Gatehouse-of-Fleet and the Linen Room, Dumfries.

Green ice cream

Cream o' Galloway ice cream has a visitor centre at Rainton, Gatehouse-of-Fleet. The organic farm has committed to using renewable energy. Find out more about their plans and eat their ice cream in the café.

www.creamogalloway.co.uk

Rare wildlife

Red Squirrels can be spotted running and jumping in the woods of Drumlanrig Castle and Country Park. Walk or hire bikes to enjoy the woodland, park and river scenery at Drumlanrig. Tours around the house give you a glimpse into the history and life of the Dukes of Buccleuch through the generations.

www.drumlanrig.com

Scottish Borders
Hidden secrets

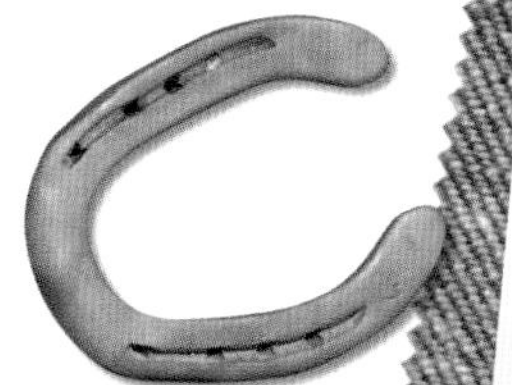

Hermitage Castle

Wooded *river valleys, and rolling green hills with a hint of wildness on the higher ground; sturdy towns with a heritage of weaving and mills; four once great abbeys, now romantically ruined; a wealth of lavish and ornate stately homes, contrasting with the Border keeps and towers that speak of local warfare long ago. Yet another theme is the horse – they say the Selkirk Common Riding is the largest mounted gathering in Europe. Then there is another surprise – a soaring, splendid sea-coast to match anything further north. Finally, with all this heritage of weaving and wool, you'll never be far from a tweed or woollens shop!*

St Abbs Harbour

UNMISSABLE

The Hume Castle stage-set

You see the outline of this fortress from miles away, so finding it (near Greenlaw) is easy. It's a pretend castle – a shell built c.1770 on an old castle site, by the local aristocrat, as a kind of giant garden ornament. Easy parking and you can walk round the ramparts. The views are totally breathtaking.

Borders seabirds

St Abbs head is probably one of Scotland's most easily accessible seabird colonies – and pretty spectacular. Park at Northfield farm on the road to the tiny village of St Abbs and it's less than half-an-hour by a good path to the lighthouse and craggy cliffs with thousands of auks and kittiwakes. (NB. Less able visitors can drive all the way) **www.ntsseabirds.org.uk**

Sea Birds at St Abbs

Mellerstain House

WORTH A LOOK

Mellerstain

If you have limited time and want a good representative of the wealth of country house architecture, then Mellerstain is especially impressive: terraced gardens below a vast Borders sky. **www.mellerstain.com**

Osprey watch near Peebles

No need to go to the Highlands. There should be two osprey watching centres (assuming the birds come back after over-wintering), at Kailzie Gardens and Glentress, signposted from Peebles town centre. **www.forestry.gov.uk/forestry/infd-68jn86**

Lammermuir viewpoints

At one point and one point only, you can see from Fife to England! It's on the B6355 Duns to Gifford road. Look for the layby. Through a gap northwards you can see the East and West Lomonds of Fife. Behind you is The Cheviot, south of the Border.

Lammermuir

River Tweed

Picnic by the Halter Burn

Mitchell's the deli in Kelso will provide the provisions, then drive south-east for Town Yetholm and Kirk Yetholm. A narrow road, up and over, leads to parking place (on left) on valley floor by the Halter Burn. Then pick your spot!

Scots wha hae wi' Wallace bled...

Sir Walter Scott has a famous viewpoint over the Tweed, north-east of St Boswells. Less well known is the giant statue of the Scots patriot William Wallace, erected nearby in 1814. Signposted from the Dryburgh road, it's an easy walk to the statue. Inevitably, also a grand panorama across the river.

Hermitage Castle

A bleak moorland and waterside setting mean this castle scores high for atmosphere. It once had an owner so unpleasant – Baron de Soulis – that the locals finally boiled him alive. You may wish to cheer yourself up with some shopping. Hawick is close by and has plenty of choice on its long main street.
www.historic-scotland.gov.uk

More to explore

Giacopazzis for fish and chips

In Eyemouth, old-established traditional fish and chip shop/ restaurant noted for its famous batter. Wander along the quayside with your takeaway and see if you can spot the seals in the harbour.

Eyemouth Golf Club

Features the most extraordinary hole in the UK – the 6th – a coastal hole played over a vast rocky inlet, spectacular at high tide.
www.visitscotland.com/golf

Philiphaugh Salmon Viewing Centre

Angling is big business in the Scottish Borders. Discover the lure here. In season, live views of fish underwater. Plenty of info on life story of salmon. Also riverside walks on estate.
www.salmonviewingcentre.com

Kelso butchers

Wylie the butchers in Kelso. Note if self-catering. Top quality local lamb and other meat products -go when it's busy, and appreciate the great banter with the locals!

Local Listings

THERE WAS ONLY EVER GOING TO BE SO MUCH WE COULD INCLUDE IN THIS GUIDE.

THAT'S WHY WE MADE THIS SPACE AVAILABLE: IT ALLOWS MANY OF SCOTLAND'S PLACES TO STAY, EAT AND VISIT TO GET A LOOK IN AND LET YOU IN ON A FEW SECRETS ABOUT WHAT THEY OFFER THEMSELVES.

READ ON AND FIND OUT MORE: FROM SPAS AND DISTILLERIES TO GOLF COURSES AND EVEN A CHOCOLATE FACTORY, THERE'S ALWAYS SOMETHING MORE FOR YOU TO DISCOVER.

Hebridean Luxury Holidays

29 Kenneth Street, Stornoway, Isle of Lewis HS1 2DR
tel: 08006 343 270 | email: info@hebrideanluxuryholidays.co.uk
www.hebrideanluxuryholidays.co.uk

Luxurious 5 star self-catering timber lodges built using environmentally sensitive methods and materials, offering everything you need for a break on Lewis. Morag is on hand to help you get the most from your holiday, with advice on car hire, food hampers and where to eat and shop. Nothing is too much trouble.

Scarista House

Scarista House, Isle of Harris HS3 3HX | tel: 01859 550 238
email: timandpatricia@scaristahouse.com | www.scaristahouse.com

Given its position on the edge of the Atlantic Ocean, it is not surprising that locally caught seafood dominates the menu at Scarista House. Lobster from the bay, scallops delivered by the diver in his diving suit and halibut which catches the 14.20 bus to be in time for dinner.

Broad Bay House

Back, Near Stornoway, Isle of Lewis HS2 0LQ | tel: 01851 820 990
email: stay@broadbayhouse.co.uk | www.broadbayhouse.co.uk

Set in a stunning beachside location, Broad Bay House provides unrivalled 5 Star accommodation and Eat Scotland silver award winning local fish, meat and game.

White Falls Spa Retreat

White Falls Spa Retreat, 2 Breasclete, Isle of Lewis HS2 9ED
tel: 01851 621 771 | email: donald@lochroag.com | www.whitefalls.co.uk

The luxurious and spacious cedar lodges offer unequalled tranquillity and the perfect setting to let you relax and unwind in your own private spa.

Tiroran House

Tiroran House, Isle of Mull PA69 6ES | tel: 01681 705 232.
email: tiroran-house@btconnect.com | www.tiroran.com

Hidden from prying eyes at the feet of Mother Nature, lovely comfortable Country House nestling on the unspoilt shores of Loch Schridain on Mull. Breathtaking views, beautifully individual en-suite bedrooms and well maintained gardens leading to the sea. Dine on local and Scottish produce used to wonderful effect. Licensed.

The Pierhouse Hotel

The Pierhouse Hotel, Port Appin, Argyll PA38 4DE | tel: 01631 730 302
email: reservations@pierhousehotel.co.uk | www.pierhousehotel.co.uk

The Pierhouse Hotel in Port Appin is a gem of a hotel with spectacular panoramic views of Loch Linnhe. One of Argyll's best kept secrets, this intimate 12 bedroom hotel and award-winning seafood restaurant has won a fast-growing reputation for its exceptional fresh local seasonal Scottish seafood, meat and game.

Cologin Country Chalets and Lodges

Cologin Country Chalets and Lodges, Cologin, Lerags Glen, Oban PA34 4SE | tel: 01631 564 501 | email: info@cologin.co.uk
www.cologin.co.uk

Hidden between rolling hills in Lerags Glen, Cologin offers a taste of tranquillity. Catch wild brown trout from our loch and we'll cook it, on-site, in our country pub/restaurant.

Oban Chocolate Company

34 Corran Esplanade, Oban, Argyll PA34 5PS | tel: 01631 566 099
email: enquiries@obanchocolate.net | www.oban-chocolate.co.uk

Step into the chocolatey world of Oban Chocolates and experience a world of innovative handmade chocolates from the fiery chilli chuffle to the sublime walnut cappuccino. All handmade by a specialist team of chocolatiers, there's also a fantastic café with beautiful views across Oban Bay.

The Isle of Eriska Hotel, Spa & Island

Ledaig, by Oban, Argyll, PA37 1SD | tel: 01631 720 371
email: office@eriska-hotel.co.uk | www.eriska-hotel.co.uk

The Isle of Eriska Hotel, Spa and Island is a unique combination of a 300 acre privately owned island, a 5 AA Red Star 25 bedroom hotel with world renowned 3 AA Rosette Restaurant and a stunning combination of outdoor activities and indoor sporting facilities with a full service Espa Spa.

Oban Distillery

Oban, Argyll PA34 5NH | tel: 01631 572 005

Oban Distillery offers guided distillery 'flavour' tours. Try Oban malt whisky with food, and direct from the cask. A discount voucher and free gift are included with admission. Malt whisky gift shop & exhibition also available. The Visitor Centre is open all year round (excluding January). For further information please call tel: 01631 572 005.

Pine Lodge Holidays

The Old School, Dalavich, Taynuilt, Argyll PA35 1HN | tel: 01866 830 049
email: contact@offthemainroad.co.uk | www.offthemainroad.co.uk

Escape to the remote beauty of Dalavich, Loch Awe. New self-catering accommodation in converted school. Free fly-fishing taster lesson available to all guests.

Highlands & Skye

The Three Chimneys & The House Over-By

The Three Chimneys & The House Over-By, Colbost, Dunvegan, Isle of Skye IV55 8ZT | tel: 01470 511 258
email: eatandstay@threechimneys.co.uk | www.threechimneys.co.uk

Scotland's renowned restaurant with rooms sits close by the sea on the road to the most westerly edge of the Isle of Skye. Its unique 'Seven Courses of Skye' dinner menu showcases the quality and freshness of the island's finest local produce. The experience cannot be replicated anywhere, worldwide.

Toravaig House Hotel

Toravaig House Hotel, Knock Bay, Sleat, Isle of Skye IV44 8RE
tel: 01471 820 200 | email: info@skyehotel.co.uk | www.skyehotel.co.uk

This is the ultimate, boutique style, romantic retreat on the Isle of Skye. Our chefs use fresh local produce to create award-winning, fine-dining, menus - Skye seafood, fresh island grown vegetables, salad leaves, soft fruits & cheeses to name a few. Daily sailing trips on board our exclusive luxury yacht from May to September.

The Cross at Kingussie

Tweed Mill Brae, Ardbroilach Road, Kingussie PH21 1LB
tel: 01540 661 166 | email: relax@thecross.co.uk | www.thecross.co.uk

A contemporary restaurant with eight comfortable bedrooms set in a converted tweed mill and situated in four acres of riverside grounds. AA three rosette dinners feature the highest quality fresh, local and seasonal produce, with top wine list. Special dinners and inclusive breaks available from £85 all year round.

The Glenview - Restaurant with rooms

The Glenview, Culnacoc, by Staffin, Isle of Skye IV51 9JH
tel: 01470 562 248 | email: enquiries@glenviewskye.co.uk
www.glenviewskye.co.uk

We are tucked away in the idyllic landscape of the north of Skye serving the best local and organic food. A relaxing gourmet stay is guaranteed.

Plockton Inn & Seafood Restaurant

Plockton Inn, Innes Street, Plockton IV52 8TW | tel: 01599 544 222
email: info@plocktoninn.co.uk | www.plocktoninn.co.uk

Local family owned and run for the last 12 years. Log fires, traditional music nights every week and local seafood specialities. All rooms recently refurbished.

Tain Golf Club

Tain Golf Club, Chapel Road, Tain, Ross-shire IV19 1JE | tel: 01862 892 314
email: info@tain-golfclub.co.uk | www.tain-golfclub.co.uk

This jewel in the crown Highland golf course overlooks the Dornoch Firth with the sea on one side and the backdrop of the mountains behind.

The Milton Restaurant

The Milton Restaurant, Crathes, Banchory AB31 5QH | tel: 01330 844 566
email: jan@themilton.co.uk | www.themilton.co.uk

The Milton (Restaurant of the Year 2007), our restaurant, spacious conservatory and riverside events marquee are suitable for a variety of events, offering exquisite cuisine and the highest level of service. Our award-winning chefs are passionate about food and have created an excellent selection of dishes using the best of Grampian's produce.

The Falls of Feugh Restaurant

Falls of Feugh Restaurant/Tea Room, Bridge of Feugh, Banchory AB31 6HX | tel: 01330 822 227 | email: taylor.ann@btconnect.com www.thefallsoffeugh.com

Located in a stunning setting on the banks of the river Feugh, this restaurant offers an extensive lunch menu which promotes fresh local produce and is cooked to a very high standard, or create your own menu. Ann and her staff provide a rare form of hospitality which gives a unique ambience.

Banchory Lodge Hotel

Banchory Lodge Hotel, Banchory AB31 4HS | tel: 01330 822 625
email: enquiries@banchorylodge.co.uk | www.banchorylodge.co.uk

To find this best loved hidden gem, drive down the tree lined entrance to find our beautiful Georgian mansion house at the confluence of the River Dee and Feugh. Fresh flowers, magnificent paintings and delightful antiques make this hotel a wonderful retreat to enjoy fine food and a homely atmosphere.

Ardeonaig Hotel & Restaurant

Ardeonaig Hotel & Restaurant, South Road, Loch Tay, Ardeonaig, Perthshire FK21 8SU | tel: 01567 820 400. email: info@ardeonaighotel.co.uk | www.ardeonaighotel.co.uk

Where else can you live it up in a luxury African-influenced Rondawel, lodge on the banks of Scotland's most spectacular lochs? Or eat Michelin-standard food surrounded by the most extensive South African wine collection in Europe? Only at Ardeonaig Hotel and Restaurant, an idyllic hideaway well worth seeking out.

The Kingdom of Fife

The Woodside Hotel

The Woodside Hotel, 78 High Street, Aberdour, Fife KY3 0SW tel: 01383 860 328 | email: reception@thewoodsidehotel.co.uk www.thewoodsidehotel.co.uk

Situated in a beautiful village, our hotel boasts a stunning stained glass ceiling salvaged from a clipper operating in the early 1900's from Scotland to Australia.

Glen Prosen Hostel

Glenprosen Hostel, Balnaboth, Kirriemuir, Angus DD8 4SA
tel: 01575 540 238/302 | email: hector@prosenhostel.co.uk
www.prosenhostel.co.uk

View the sunset and a panorama of hills from our barbecue hut. The secret Glens of Angus have a huge variety of wildlife including red squirrel, otter, deer and black game. Glen Prosen Hostel is "the best hostel we've ever stayed in", also comfortable, traditional, self-catering riverside and moorland cottages.

The Hideaway

The Hideaway, Balkello Farm, Auchterhouse, by Dundee DD3 0RA
tel: 07939 948 796 | email: thehideaway@balkello.com
www.balkello.com

Romantic hideaway offering complete privacy and peace with a sauna, double jacuzzi bath, wood-burning stove, and four-poster bed. All only five minutes away from Dundee. Enjoy massage treatments, services of a chef, and local food boxes delivered without leaving the doorstep. Complimentary wine and home baking is also on offer.

Castleton House Hotel

Castleton House Hotel, by Glamis, Angus DD8 1SJ | tel: 01307 840 340
email: hotel@castletonglamis.co.uk | www.castletonglamis.co.uk

Castleton is a privately run country house hotel with an enviable reputation for superb food, ambience and service. Non-residents welcome. Serves lunch and dinner daily.

The Boathouse

The Boathouse, Dundas Castle, South Queensferry EH30 9SP
tel: 0131 319 2039 | email: boathouse@dundascastle.co.uk
www.dundascastle.co.uk

The luxurious 4 star Boathouse is secluded in the heart of Dundas Estate. This romantic one bedroomed cottage has beautiful views over a private loch allowing you to wake up to a champagne breakfast on the veranda whilst watching a myriad of wild birds including herons and coots.

Glasgow & the Clyde Valley

New Lanark Mill Hotel

New Lanark Mill Hotel, Mill Number One, New Lanark Mills,
Lanark ML11 9DB | tel: 01555 667 200 | email: hotel@newlanark.org
www.newlanark.org

Unlike any other in Scotland, the New Lanark Mill Hotel was originally an 18th-century cotton mill. Located within the unique setting of New Lanark World Heritage Site the hotel offers fantastic views across the surrounding conservation area and is close to the famous Falls of Clyde.

Carlton George Hotel

Carlton George Hotel, 44 West George Street, Glasgow G2 1DH
tel: 0141 353 6373 | email: resgeorge@carltonhotels.co.uk
www.carltonhotels.co.uk/george

Glasgow's premier boutique hotel, the Carlton George is located in the heart of the city centre. The hotel is a picture of sophistication and style with beautifully decorated bedrooms, rooftop restaurant and an executive lounge. The hotel is within walking distance of the business district, fabulous shopping and numerous cultural attractions.

Carmichael Country Cottages

Carmichael Country Cottages, Carmichael Estate Office, Biggar ML12 6PG
tel: 01899 308 336 | email: chiefcarm@aol.com | www.carmichael.co.uk

Scotland's oldest (1292) family farm has gorgeous stone cottages hidden in deer parks. £20 voucher to use in our farm shop for zero food-mile meats.

Scottish Borders

Peter Scott & Co

11 Buccleuch Street, Hawick TD9 0HJ | tel: 01450 364 815
email: shop@peterscott.co.uk | www.peterscott.co.uk

Independent Scottish knitwear manufacturers invite you on a free guided tour of their factory, where the finest handcrafted garments have been produced for over a century. See first hand the skills that have been passed down through the generations and have kept the local industry and community alive.

To plan your Perfect Day in Scotland, have a look at
www.visitscotland.com/perfectday
...for lots of ideas.
There's loads and loads of stuff to find out about Scotland [plus any accommodation needs], at **www.visitscotland.com** or call **0845 22 55 121** to speak to an advisor.

Calendar of events

2009 – SCOTLAND'S FIRST EVER HOMECOMING YEAR – CREATED AND TIMED TO MARK THE 250TH ANNIVERSARY OF THE BIRTH OF SCOTLAND'S NATIONAL POET, THE INTERNATIONAL CULTURAL ICON, ROBERT BURNS.

A SPECIAL YEAR FOR ALL SCOTS AND THOSE WHO LOVE SCOTLAND. A COUNTRY-WIDE PROGRAMME OF EXCITING AND INSPIRATIONAL HOMECOMING EVENTS AND ACTIVITIES: CELEBRATING BURNS HIMSELF, WHISKY, GOLF, GREAT SCOTTISH MINDS AND INNOVATIONS WITH HUNDREDS OF HERITAGE AND CULTURAL EVENTS.

WWW.HOMECOMINGSCOTLAND2009.COM

NB:

H = Homecoming '09 event

January 2009

Burning of the Clavie — *11 Jan*

Traditional fire festival celebrated every year - one of the most bizarre of Scotland's Hogmanay festivals.
Burghead, Elgin

Burns' 250th Anniversary Weekend — *24 - 25 Jan*

Official start of Homecoming 2009; highlights include the official Homecoming Burns Supper in Ayrshire. H
Venues across Scotland | www.homecomingscotland2009.com

Celtic Connections Celebrations — *24 Jan - 1 Feb*

An international celebration of the best traditional and contemporary music with Celtic roots. H
Glasgow | www.homecomingscotland2009.com

Up Helly Aa — *27 Jan*

Pagan fire festival welcoming the return of the sun.
Shetland | www.visitshetland.com

February 2009

Annual Snowdrop Festival — *1 Feb - 15 Mar*

Various events celebrating our enchanting Scottish snowdrops.
Venues across Scotland | www.white.visitscotland.com/snowdrops

New Territories — *11 Feb - 21 Mar*

Scotland's international festival of live arts.
Glasgow | www.newmoves.co.uk

Glasgow Film Festival — *12 - 22 Feb*

Showcase of films from around the world.
www.glasgowfilmfestival.org.uk

March 2009

Osprey Observation — *Beginning in Mar*

Ospreys arrive in the last week in March and lay eggs a month later. Watch them from Loch of the Lowes, near Dunkeld.
Perthshire | www.perthshire.co.uk

Aye Write! The Bank of Scotland Book Festival — *6 - 14 Mar*

Annual literature festival honouring the best Scottish and international writers. H
Glasgow | www.homecomingscotland2009.com

Scots Music Abroad — *6 Mar - 23 May*

This free exhibition exploring the worldwide legacy of Scots music from Handel to Blues and Soul. Continues throughout April into May. H
Edinburgh | www.homecomingscotland2009.com

Stanza: Scotland's Poetry Festival — *18 - 22 Mar*

Scotland's only established festival devoted to poetry: hear world class poets read to packed houses in atmospheric venues. H
St Andrews, Fife | www.homecomingscotland2009.com

Hawick Reivers Festival — *27 - 29 Mar*

A festival of fire and steel commemorating the confrontations between England and Scotland in the Border regions.
Scottish Borders | www.hawickreivers.com

The Trossachs Outdoor festival — *28 - 29 Mar*

Festival offering fantastic opportunities in the surrounding area for enjoying the great outdoors.
Trossachs | www.visitaberfoyle.com

Mauchline Plough Match — *29 Mar*

A ploughing match organised by Mauchline Burns Club honouring Burns' immortalisation of the Scottish countryside and humble farm life. H
Mauchline, Ayrshire | www.homecomingscotland2009.com

April 2009

The John Muir Odyssey — *1 Apr - 30 Jun*

A new festival celebrating the life and legacy of John Muir, a founder of National Parks and one of the most influential people in the world of environmental movement.

Throughout East Lothian | www.homecomingscotland2009.com

Tartan Day — *6 Apr*

Annual celebrations which mark the signing of the Declaration of Arbroath.

Events throughout Scotland | www.homecomingscotland2009.com

Peebles Jazz Festival — *29 Apr - 13 May*

Now in its 15th year, events take place in various local venues.

The Scottish Borders | www.peeblesjazzfestival.co.uk

Shetland Folk Festival — *30 Apr - 3 May*

UK's most northerly folk festival is a prestigious event for performers, locals and visitors alike.

Shetland | www.shetlandfolkfestival.com

Links Market Street Fair — *TBC*

Reputedly the longest street fair in Europe, running almost one mile in length along the Esplanade, Kirkcaldy.

Kirkcaldy, Fife

Shetland Folk Festival

May 2009

Scottish Mining Mayfest — *1 - 4 May*

Events, songs, music & dance marking the mining heritage and worldwide influence.
Venues across Midlothian | www.homecomingscotland2009.com

Spirit of Speyside Whisky Festival — *1 - 10 May*

Dufftown-based festival featuring craft fayre, whisky auction, tasting programme, distillery tours, dinners and the famous Dregs Party.
Dufftown | www.homecomingscotland2009.com

Whisky Month — *1 - 31 May*

An invitation to explore and appreciate the expertise and diligence of the nation's stillsmen and master blenders.
Venues across Scotland | www.homecomingscotland2009.com

Big in Falkirk — *2 -3 May*

Since its inception in 2000, this National Street Arts Festival has become one of the largest cultural events in Scotland.
Callendar Park, Falkirk | www.biginfalkirk.com

Culloden – From Battle to Exile — *9 - 10 May*

A weekend programme of events telling the story of the battle, its aftermath and the journey to a new life overseas.
By Inverness | www.homecomingscotland2009.com

Loch Lomond Quilt Show — *20 - 23 May*

An inspiring showcase of Scotland's unique textile heritage.
Venues from Loch Lomond to Dumbarton

Perth Festival of the Arts — *21 - 31 May*

11-day international arts festival which includes orchestral music, opera, jazz, folk, visual art and more.
Perth Concert Hall | www.perthfestival.co.uk

May 2009 (cont.)

Party at the Palace 1503 — 23 - 24 May

Celebration of the Stewart Royal Court at Linlithgow Palace. H
Linlithgow Palace, Linlithgow
www.homecomingscotland2009.com

Doune / Dunblane Fling — 30 - 31 May

An annual festival originally founded with the local community in mind however, it has begun to grow and attract visitors far and wide. H
Venues around Doune and Dunblane | www.dunblanefling.com
www.homecomingscotland2009.com

Emirates Airline Edinburgh Sevens — 30 - 31 May

7's rugby was invented in Scotland and is played worldwide. Final leg of the IRB Word Sevens Series. H
Murrayfield Stadium, Edinburgh
www.homecomingscotland2009.com

Arran Wildlife Festival — TBC

Spectacular and accessible Arran offers a wealth of wildlife; this festival aims to encourage visitors to enjoy it in a sustainable way.
Arran | www.arranwildlife.co.uk

British and Scottish Gold Panning Championships — TBC

Gold is found in the sand and gravel in the burns around Wanlockhead, home of the annual gold panning championships.
Dumfries & Galloway

Peebles Beltane Festival

June 2009

Balquhidder Summer Music Festival — *Jun - Aug*

This long-running festival hosts an eclectic mix of professional musicians.
Trossachs

Bruce Festival — *1 - 30 Jun*

Celebration of King Robert the Bruce.
Pittencrieff Park, Dunfermline I *www.visitdunfermline.com*

Taste of Grampian — *6 Jun*

Discover and sample the wide range of high quality food and drink products from the area.
Inverurie, Aberdeenshire I *www.tasteofgrampian.co.uk*

The Crossing — *14 - 21 Jun*

Celebration marking the Caledonian Canal's place in the story of the Scottish Enlightenment. H
Caledonian Canal, Highlands
www.homecomingscotland2009.com

Edinburgh International Film Festival — *17 - 28 Jun*

World-renowned film festival; Homecoming year sees films by Scottish filmmakers and discusses Scottish influence on film-making. H
Venues across Edinburgh I *www.homecomingscotland2009.com*

Johnsmas Foy — *18 - 28 Jun*

Shetland's midsummer festival that marks the arrival of Dutch herring fleet in the islands and features an exciting line-up of local and international acts. *NB: mid-summer months in Shetland also have up to 19 hours of daylight!*
Shetland I *www.johnsmasfoy.com*

Ceres Highland Games — *TBC*

The oldest free games in Scotland: a cheerful mix of pipe music, dancing, and competition.
Ceres, Fife I *www.ceresgames.co.uk*

CLAN GATHERINGS

June 2009 (cont.)

DOUNE GALA — *TBC*

Starts around midday, led by a pipe band to the village and lasts until evening; a 'duck race' is run the following day.
Doune, Trossachs

PEEBLES BELTANE FESTIVAL — *TBC*

A festival of local legend and tradition marking the return of summer with the lighting of fires.
Peebles, Scottish Borders | www.peeblesbeltanefestival.co.uk

July 2009

THE SCOTTISH TRADITIONAL BOAT FESTIVAL — *2 - 5 July*

Over four days, explore your roots and take part in a colourful celebration of Scotland's great maritime heritage.
Portsoy, Aberdeenshire | www.homecomingscotland2009.com

GAME CONSERVANCY SCOTTISH FAIR — *3 - 5 July*

Gundog, fishing and shooting competitions with outdoor activities including archery, fly casting and quad bikes.
Scone Palace, Perthshire | www.scottishfair.com

ALVA HIGHLAND GAMES — *11 July*

At 152 years old, the longest standing Highland Games in Clackmannanshire with full range of traditional events.
Alva, Stirlingshire | www.alva.ukctest.co.uk

The Open Golf Championship — 16 - 19 July

The Open Championship comes to Turnberry - a focal point of the year of Homecoming.
Ailsa Course, Turnberry | *www.homecomingscotland2009.com*

Art On The Map — 17 July - 16 Aug

Local artists capture and bring alive the sites, landscape and life of the Outer Hebrides.
Throughout the Western Isles
www.homecomingscotland2009.com

Inverness Highland Games — 18 - 19 July

Established in 1822, one of the most spectacular Games in the Scottish Highlands.
Inverness | *www.homecomingscotland2009.com*

Big Tent Festival — 25 - 26 July

Environmental festival celebrating cultural revival and positive action featuring a line-up of world and folk music.
Falkland, Fife | *www.bigtentfestival.co.uk*

The Gathering — 25 -26 July

Largest clan gathering in history, with parades, Highland Games and plenty of history.
Edinburgh | *www.homecomingscotland2009.com*

Guildtown Bluegrass Music Festival 2009 — 31 July - 3 Aug

Scotland's only Bluegrass music festival extends a special welcome to international visitors.
Guildtown Village Hall, near Perth
www.homecomingscotland2009.com

August 2009

TURRIFF SHOW — *2 - 3 AUG*

Probably Scotland's largest two-day agricultural show attracting local and overseas visitors.
Aberdeen | www.turriffshow.org

CREATIVE CONNECTIONS — *3 - 9 AUG*

Fiddling, arts and crafts and storytelling, inspired by Shetland's remote location, and distinctive heritage. H
Shetland | www.homecomingscotland2009.com

BELLADRUM TARTAN HEART FESTIVAL — *7 - 8 AUG*

A family-friendly weekend festival of music and performing arts, reuniting Homecoming Highlanders in spectacular surroundings. H
Belladrum Estate, Beauly | www.homecomingscotland2009.com

TATTOO HEBRIDES 2009 — *7 - 8 AUG*

Stornoway's two-day Hebridean Ceilidh and Lewis Highland Games with military Tattoo performed by 7 pipe bands. H
Throughout Stornoway | www.homecomingscotland2009.com

AYR FLOWER SHOW — *7 - 9 AUG*

Scotland's premier horticultural event, often referred to as the Chelsea of the North. H
Ayr, South Ayrshire | www.homecomingscotland2009.com

EDINBURGH INTERNATIONAL FESTIVAL — *14 AUG - 6 SEPT*

Scotland's largest arts festival. H
Venues across Edinburgh | www.homecomingscotland2009.com

WORLD PIPE BAND CHAMPIONSHIPS — *15 AUG*

A day of vibrant colours, music and competition: 8,000 pipes and drums, 200 bands, but only 1 world champion. H
Glasgow Green, Glasgow | www.homecomingscotland2009.com

Kirkintilloch Canal Festival — *24 - 31 Aug*

Celebration with a focus on the creation of Scottish Canals and their use around the world.
Forth and Clyde Canal, Kirkintilloch
www.homecomingscotland2009.com

Connect Music Festival — *28 - 30 Aug*

The finest gourmet food and drink in stunning countryside, with big name stars and bands. *Inverary Castle, Inverary, Argyll*
www.homecomingscotland2009.com

Cowal Gathering — *29 Aug*

An international extravaganza to enjoy dancers, food and local produce, music, street theatre and massed bands and pipes.
Argyll & Bute | www.homecomingscotland2009.com

St. Kilda Day: Latha Hiort — *29 Aug - 30 Sept*

Marks the evacuation of St Kilda in 1930 celebrating St. Kildans' lives and legacy in music, word and image.
Across Scotland | www.homecomingscotland2009.com

World Pipe Band Championships

Hawick Summer Festival

August 2009 (cont.)

Arbroath Seafest — *TBC*

Annually celebrates the sea and Angus' strong links and age old dependency on the sea.
Arbroath, Angus | www.angusahead.com

Culross Festival — *TBC*

Includes opera, blues, folk music, drama and dance concluding with a Medieval Burgh Fair.
Culross, Fife | www.culrossfestival.com

Hawick Summer Festival — *TBC*

Discover the beauties and bounties of the Borders, a paradise for walkers, cyclists and historians.
Hawick, Scottish Borders

Scottish Alternative Games — *TBC*

A quirky take on traditional highland games with gird and cleek racing, tossing the sheaf and hurlin' the curlin' stane.
Castle Douglas | www.scottish-alternative-games.com

Scribblers Picnic — *TBC*

A charity set up in 2001 to raise money for cancer charities, with four stages of music and a fete.
Stirling | www.scribblerspicnic.com

Trossachs Beer Festival — *TBC*

Traditional beer festival with live folk music, beer-related events and a special menu throughout the week.
Callendar, Perthshire

Connect Festival

September 2009

Doors Open Day — ***Throughout Sept***

Get behind-the-scenes of some of Scotland's best-loved and least-known architectural gems.
Throughout Scotland | www.homecomingscotland2009.com

Blas Festival – Celebrating the Highlands — ***4 - 12 Sept***

An authentic flavour of Highland culture with traditional music and events in spectacular landscapes.

Across the Highlands | www.homecomingscotland2009.com

Clackmannanshire Walking Festival — ***7 - 8 Sept***

Magnificent scenery and interesting wildlife walks over hills and through woodland and 'built heritage' trails.
Stirling | www.clacksweb.org.uk

Isle of Barra Whisky Galore Festival — ***18 - 20 Sept***

Take part in the hunt for whisky, chat with the locals or participate in the golf tournament.
Isle of Barra, Outer Hebrides
www.homecomingscotland2009.com

The Stenaline Wigtown Book Festival — ***25 Sept - 4 Oct***

Talks and tastings celebrating literature's long love affair with whisky, with a welcome home for the Ulster Scots.
Throughout Wigtown | www.homecomingscotland2009.com

East Lothian Food & Drink Festival — ***25 - 27 Sept***

Celebrating the country's fine food and drink traditions with an exciting and varied programme of events.
East Lothian | www.foodanddrinkeastlothian.com

Angus & Dundee Roots Festival — ***26 Sept- 5 Oct***

An opportunity for people whose ancestors came from the area to find out about their ancestral homeland.
Throughout Angus and Dundee
www.homecomingscotland2009.com

September 2009 (cont.)

Arran Outdoor Festival *TBC*

Experience the 7 wonders of Arran (mountains, coastline, adventure activities, food and drink, music, well-being and relaxation, wildlife.
Arran, Ayrshire | www.arranoutdoorfestival.co.uk

Callander Jazz & Blues Festival *TBC*

A long weekend of live music at venues throughout this National Park gateway town.
Trossachs | www.callanderjazz.com

Dundee Flower & Food Festival *TBC*

The premier show of its kind in Scotland: a three-day menu of food, flowers and fun.
Camperdown Park | www.dundeeflowerandfoodfestival.com

Trossachs Real Ale Festival *TBC*

Up to 30 different beers and ales to try, with live entertainment and good food.
Trossachs

Royal National Mod, Isle of Lewis

Samhain Festival

October 2009

The Royal National Mod — 9 - 17 Oct

Scotland's premier Gaelic language, music and culture showcase comes home to Oban.
Oban, Argyll | *www.homecomingscotland2009.com*

Glasgow: The Beautiful Journey — 15 - 31 Oct

Reflecting the Clyde's history through stunning visual imagery, fire and music. Launches a new 'ship' every night.
Glasgow | *www.homecomingscotland2009.com*

Highland Homecoming — 15 - 31 Oct

Fortnight-long series of events that explores the way Scots have shaped countries and communities around the world.
Across the Highlands | *www.homecomingscotland2009.com*

The Enchanted Forest Pitlochry Autumn Festival — 16 Oct - 1 Nov

See autumn colours in abundance and enjoy street festivals, busking musicians and ghost tours.
Pitlochry, Perthshire | *www.homecomingscotland2009.com*

Celebrate Linlithgow — 16 Oct - 1 Nov

A festival by and for the townspeople discovering the diversity of local arts.
Linlithgow | *www.celebrate-linlithgow.org.uk*

Samhain Festival — 31 Oct

Samhain or 'Summer's End' is the Celtic Festival which some say marked the Celtic New Year.
Kenmore, Perthshire

Aberfoyle International Mushroom Festival — TBC

A festival of fungi, food, drink and music. Annual themes have included Viking, Maori and Irish flavours.
Trossachs | *www.visitaberfoyle.com*

For more events go to www.visitscotland.com

November 2009

Craigmillar Castle Park — Throughout Nov

See buzzards and kestrels soaring overhead throughout the month.
Edinburgh

St. Andrews Festival 2009 – Scotland's Celebration — 23 - 30 Nov

Celebration of the Patron Saint; with premiere of a spectacular 'son et lumiere' of Scottish history, projected onto the town's medieval walls.
St Andrews, Fife | www.homecomingscotland2009.com

Homecoming Scotland's Finale Weekend — 28 - 30 Nov

Celebrations on a scale never seen before, encompassing the fullest possible range of Scotland's popular musicians at home and abroad.
Across Scotland | www.homecomingscotland2009.com

December 2009

Bringing in the New Year — 31 Dec

Hogmanay is always celebrated throughout Scotland in style... and all a bit differently. The main cities tend to go big (**Edinburgh** & **Glasgow** are examples of huge parties) while locally you'll find unique ways of welcoming in 2010; **Comrie's Flambeaux Procession** with its torchlights to drive evil spirits from the village and the colourful **Stonehaven Fireballs Festival** both good examples.

Burning the Clavie, Moray

Top 10's
Scotland's best

We asked experts from all disciplines to name the top ten Scottish attractions in their field: and the results are in!

Top 10
Pub musicians' favourite haunts

The thing about traditional music in Scotland is it's traditional to have a pint afterwards. Fiddlers, guitarists, bodhran players and singers all tell us where they wet their whistle.

1. THE DOG HOUSE, LOCH LOMOND
2. THE ROYAL OAK, EDINBURGH
3. BUTTERFLY & PIG, GLASGOW
4. MIDCALDER INN, EDINBURGH & LOTHIANS
5. THE LOUNGE, LERWICK
6. THE BLUE LAMP, ABERDEEN
7. THE GLOBE, ABERDEEN
8. THE FOUNDRY BAR, ARBROATH
9. THE TAYBANK, DUNKELD
10. ROLLING HILLS FOLK CLUB, MELROSE

'...these are pubs with great atmospheres which make musicians & singers feel right at home.'
KAY THOMSON, MUSICIAN

Top 10
Fishermen's best fish & chip shops

Even for the best, there are days where one or two get away. When that happens, find out where Scotland's fishermen like to go for the finest fish and chips.

1. ASHVALE, BRECHIN
2. THE BERVIE CHIPPER, INVERBERVIE
3. THE DOLPHIN CAFÉ, PETERHEAD FISH MARKET
4. THE GEORGE STREET CHIPPY, OBAN
5. LAND AND SEA, POLMONT
6. ANSTRUTHER FISH BAR, ANSTRUTHER
7. THE TOWNHEAD CAFE, BIGGAR
8. ZANDERS, PETERHEAD
9. DUNKELD TRADITIONAL FISH BAR, DUNKELD
10. SEA FORTH CHIPPY, ULLAPOOL

'After a drive in the Scottish countryside, there's nothing better than stopping for a fish supper... especially from the Ashvale'

JIM SWANKIE, SKIPPER, ARBROATH

Top 10

Caddies' favourite golf courses

Where would a Scottish caddie play on his day off? We know, because we asked them. Share in their insider knowledge and pick up some tips into the bargain.

'Scotland's golf courses are second to none, for me, Machrihanish lives up to its exalted billing as you tee up on the greatest first hole in the world of golf.'

JOHN BOYNE, CADDIE, ST ANDREWS OLD COURSE

1. **MACHRIHANISH GOLF CLUB,** MULL OF KINTYRE
2. **FRASERBURGH GOLF CLUB,** ABERDEEN & GRAMPIAN
3. **BOAT OF GARTEN GOLF CLUB,** HIGHLANDS
4. **FORTROSE & ROSEMARKIE,** HIGHLANDS
5. **SHISKINE GOLF CLUB (12 HOLES),** ARRAN
6. **BRORA GOLF CLUB,** HIGHLANDS
7. **DUNAVERTY GOLF COURSE,** SOUTHWEST
8. **MONTROSE GOLF COURSE,** ANGUS & DUNDEE
9. **SOUTHERNESS GOLF COURSE,** DUMFRIES & GALLOWAY
10. **STONEHAVEN GOLF CLUB,** ABERDEEN & GRAMPIAN

Top 10
Designers' favourite boutiques

What's cool and what's old school? Better still, where do leading Scottish designers go to pick up cool things and get inspirational new ideas? You saw it here first.

1. BRAZEN STUDIOS, GLASGOW
2. NUMBER 46, BALLATER (NEAR BALMORAL)
3. FLORAIDH, ISLE OF SKYE.
4. SHANAZIA, GLASGOW
5. TOTTY ROCKS, EDINBURGH
6. DESIGN HOUSE, ABERDEEN
7. OUT OF THE BLUE STUDIOS, EDINBURGH
8. LINTON HOUSE, NAIRN
9. ART ROOM 59, DUNFERMLINE
10. ARTERY GALLERY, ST ANDREWS

'We are spoiled for choice when it comes to finding a quality design store in Scotland, Totty Rocks is one which has beautiful locally designed clothes and accessories.'

KATHERINE EMTAGE,
HAND CRAFTED BAG DESIGNER

Top 10
'Stonemasons' favourite buildings

Stonemasons know a thing or two about architectural beauty. Here's their list of the top ten Scottish buildings, so you can see who's carving a name for themselves.

1. **The Pack Horse Bridge,** Stow
2. **The Ballochmyle Viaduct,** nr Mauchline, Ayrshire
3. **Parthenon Frieze Plaster Casts,** Edinburgh College of Art
4. **Andrew Lamb's House,** Leith
5. **The Pineapple,** Dunmore
6. **The National Wallace Monument,** Stirling
7. **Glasgow City Centre,** Victorian ornamental architectural adornment
8. **Edinburgh New Town,** Georgian Architecture
9. **Aberdeen City centre,** granite
10. **Bell Rock Lighthouse,** 11 miles off of Arbroath

'Scotland has a plethora of fantastic buildings and the Bell Rock Lighthouse is one of the greatest engineering feats of the industrial age.'

Colin Tennant, Stonemason

Top 10
Rangers' wildlife hotspots

Nature guides are almost as flighty as the animals they observe. But we did manage to get a few recommendations of where to go for some wonderful sights. Shhhhhhh!

1. **OSPREY,** DAVID MARSHALL LODGE (QUEEN ELIZABETH FOREST PARK, BY ABERFOYLE); GLENTRESS FOREST; KAILZIE GARDENS NEAR PEEBLES
2. **PEREGRINE,** HUNTLY PEREGRINE WATCH, HUNTLY
3. **WHITE TAILED SEA EAGLE,** LOCH FRISA, ISLE OF MULL; HEN HARRIER KILMORY WILDLIFE VIEWING PROJECT; ISLE OF ARRAN
4. **OTTER,** CULBIN OTTER POOL, CULBIN FOREST; MORAY & KYLERHEA HIDE, KYLERHEA; ISLE OF SKYE
5. **BAT,** CULBIN FOREST; MORAY & GLENTROOL; GALLOWAY
6. **RED SQUIRREL,** ROSEISLE; MORAY & KNAPDALE FOREST; WEST ARGYLL
7. **RED & ROE DEER,** PLODDA WOOD, FORT AUGUSTUS
8. **PINEMARTEN,** GLENMORE FOREST PARK (BY AVIEMORE); DALCHORK FOREST, NEAR DORNOCH
9. **DOLPHINS,** MORAY FIRTH, FROM HILL 99 TOWER; CULBIN FOREST
10. **BUTTERFLIES,** NATURE RESERVE, MABIE FOREST, NEAR DUMFRIES; SUNART OAKWOODS, LOCHABER

'There's real variety of wildlife in Scotland, on the way to Culbin Forest's viewing tower, visit the Dragonfly Pool and Gravel Pit Ponds for many other species.'

LAURA STEWART, FORESTRY COMMISSION RANGER

THE
GLENROTHES
ESTD LIMITED RELEASE 1879
SINGLE SPEYSIDE MALT
Scotch Whisky

Getting here

Planes, trains and automobiles

By Plane

Flybe offers frequent flights to Scotland from London Gatwick and Southampton with a choice of direct routes to Aberdeen, Inverness, Edinburgh and Glasgow. Take an onward connection to a range of destinations across the Highlands and Islands with flights operated by Flybe's franchise partner Loganair.

Flybe is the low fare airline with a difference; offering a generous frequent flyer programme open to all passengers, online check in, pre-allocated seating and more legroom.

Flights available to book now from as little as £27.99 one way on **www.flybe.com**

By Train

Getting to Scotland by train couldn't be easier. There are now direct daily services to Scotland from almost every major train station in England. From Doncaster to Dundee or Portsmouth to Perth, there are a number of train operators to choose from. Simply contact National Rail Enquiries to find out more - 08457 48 49 50 or **www.nationalrail.co.uk**

By Automobile

Scotland is easily accessible by car. From the south you can use the M1, passing through on to the M6 before entering the A74 into Scotland. Alternatively, why not take the A7 via Carlisle where you can explore the scenic 'back' roads into the Scottish Borders. You can also enjoy a drive up the East Coast on the A1.

The Visitor Information Centre Directory

There are over 107 Visitor Information Centres throughout Scotland, and with 70 of them open all year round, there's no doubt one will be close by wherever you are to help you make the most of your visit.

All our Visitor Information Centres are packed with information on things to see and do, places to visit and handy hints on what simply can't be missed in the area. However the most valuable thing about each centre has to be the friendly and knowledgeable staff on hand to help you get the most out of your time here.

You can benefit from their personal experiences and specialist local knowledge. They can point you to the best attractions, restaurants and bars, find you accommodation and tell you more about the area than could ever possibly be printed!

For an online directory with maps and directions to help you locate your nearest centre go to **www.visitscotland.com/wheretofindus**

And we have another treat in store; we've teamed up with The Glenrothes Malt Whisky to offer the first 50 people who visit 5 or more Visitor Information Centres, **a free bottle of the Glenrothes Select Reserve.** For more information and terms and conditions turn to p132 of this guide.

Aberdeen & Grampian
www.aberdeen-grampian.com

- **Aberdeen** 23 Union Street, Aberdeen, AB11 5BP tel: 01224 288828 *Open All Year*
- **Alford** Old Station Yard, Alford, AB33 8FD tel: 019755 62052 Seasonal Openings *(17 Mar - 28 Sept)*
- **Ballater** The Old Royal Station, Station Square, Ballater, AB35 5QB tel: 013397 55306 *Open All Year*
- **Banchory** Bridge Street, Banchory, AB31 5SX tel: 01330 822000 Seasonal Openings *(17 Mar - 25 Oct)*
- **Banff** Collie Lodge, Banff, AB45 1AU tel: 01261 812419 Seasonal Openings *(17 Mar - 25 Oct)*
- **Braemar** Unit 3, The Mews, Mar Road, Braemar, AB35 5YL tel: 013397 41600 *Open All Year*
- **Crathie** Car Park, Craithie, AB35 5UL tel: 013397 42414 *Open All Year*
- **Fraserburgh** 3 Saltoun Square, Fraserburgh, AB43 5DS tel: 01346 518315 *Seasonal Openings (17 Mar - 25 Oct)*
- **Huntly** 9A The Square, Huntly, AB54 8BR tel: 01466 792255 Seasonal Openings *(17 Mar - 25 Oct)*
- **Inverurie** 18 High Street, Inverurie, AB51 3XQ tel: 01467 625800 Seasonal Openings *(17 Mar - 25 Oct)*
- **Stonehaven** 66 Allardice Street, Stonehaven, AB39 9ET tel: 01569 762806 Seasonal Openings *(17 Mar - 25 Oct)*

Pony Trekking at Balmoral Castle

Angus and Dundee
www.angusanddundee.co.uk

- **Arbroath** Harbour Visitor Centre, Fishmarket Quay, Arbroath, DD11 1PS tel: 01241 872609 *Open All Year*
- **Brechin** Pictavia Centre, Haughmuir, Brechin tel: 01356 623050 *Open All Year*
- **Dundee** Discovery Quay, Riverside Drive, Dundee, DD1 4XA tel: 01382 527527 *Open All Year*

Brechin Shopping

Argyll, the Isles, Loch Lomond, Stirling and Trossachs
www.visitscottishheartlands.com

- **Aberfoyle** Trossachs Discovery Centre, Main Street, Aberfoyle, FK8 3UQ tel: 01887 382352 *Open all year (weekends only off-peak)*
- **Ardgartan** by Arrochar, G83 7AR tel: 01301 702432 Seasonal Openings *(10 Mar - 31 Oct)*
- **Balloch** The Old Station Building, Balloch, G83 8LQ I tel: 01389 753533 *Seasonal Openings (1 Apr - 5 Oct, all open 7 days)*
- **Bo'ness** Bo'ness Station, Union Street, Bo'ness, G83 8LQ tel: 01506 826626 Seasonal Openings *(Mar - Jan)*
- **Bowmore** The Square, Bowmore, Isle of Islay, PA43 7JP tel: 01496 810254 *Open All Year*
- **Callander** Ancaster Square, Callander, FK17 8ED tel: 01877 330342 *Open All year*
- **Campbeltown** Mackinnon House, The Pier, Campbeltown, PA28 6EF tel: 01586 552056 *Open All Year*

- **Craignure** The Pier, Craignure, Isle of Mull, PA65 6AY tel: 01680 812377 *Open All Year (times may vary based on ferry variations)*
- **Dumbarton** Milton, A82 North Bound, G82 2TZ tel: 01389 742306 *Seasonal Openings (4 Apr - 26 Oct)*
- **Dunoon** 7 Alexander Place, Dunoon, PA23 8AB tel: 01369 703785 *Open All Year*
- **Falkirk** The Falkirk Wheel, Lime Road, Tamfourhill, Falkirk, FK1 4RS tel: 01324 620244 *Open All Year*
- **Helensburgh** The Clock Tower, Helensburgh, G84 7PA tel: 01436 672642 *Seasonal Openings (4 Apr- 26 Oct)*
- **Inveraray** Front Street, Inveraray, PA32 8UY tel: 01499 302063 *Open All Year*
- **Killin** Breadalbane Folklore Centre, Main Street, Killin, FK21 8XE tel: 01567 820254 *Seasonal Openings (1 Apr- 31 Oct)*
- **Lochgilphead** Lochnell Street, Lochgilphead, PA31 8JL tel: 01546 602344 *Seasonal Openings (4 Apr - 26 Oct)*
- **Oban** Argyll Square, Oban, PA34 4AR tel: 01631 563122 *Open All Year*
- **Stirling** 41 Dumbarton Road, Stirling, FK8 2LQ tel: 01786 475019 *Open All Year*
- **Stirling (Pirnhall)** Motorway Service Area, Junction 9, M9 tel: 01786 814111 *Open All Year*
- **Rothesay** Winter Gardens, Rothesay, Isle of Bute, PA20 0AJ tel: 01700 502151 *Open All Year*
- **Strontian** Stontian, Acharacle, Argyll, PH36 4HZ tel: 01967 402381 *Seasonal Openings (21 Mar - 18 Oct)*
- **Tarbet (Loch Fyne)** Harbour Street, Tarbet, PA29 6UD tel: 01880 820429 *Seasonal Openings (4 Apr - 26 Oct)*
- **Tarbet (Loch Lomond)** Main Street, Tarbet, G83 7DE tel: 01301 702260 *Seasonal Openings (4 Apr - 26 Oct)*
- **Tillicoultry** Unit 22, Sterling Mills Outlet Village, Devondale, Tillicoultry, Clackmannanshire, FK13 6HQ tel 01259 769696 *Open All year*
- **Tobermory** The Pier, Tobermory, Isle of Mull, PA75 6NU tel: 01688 302182 *Seasonal Openings (4 Apr - 26 Oct)*
- **Tyndrum** Main Street, Tyndrum, FK20 8RY tel: 01838 400324 *Seasonal Openings (31 Mar - 22 Oct)*

Ayrshire & Arran
www.ayrshire-arran.com

- **Ayr** 22 Sandgate, Ayr, KA7 1BW tel: 01292 290300 *Open All Year*
- **Brodick** The Pier, Brodick, Isle of Arran, KA27 8AU tel: 01770 303774 *Open All Year*
- **Largs** The Railway Station, Main Street, Largs, KA30 8AN tel: 01475 689962 *Seasonal Openings (20 Mar - 18 Oct)*

Isle of Arran Distillery

Golf at Kelso

Scottish Borders
www.scot-borders.co.uk

- **Eyemouth** Auld Kirk, Manse Road, Eyemouth, TD14 5JE tel: 01890 750678 *Seasonal Openings (20 Mar - 31 Oct)*
- **Hawick** Tower Mill, Hawick, TD9 0AE tel: 01450 373993 *Open All Year (Various opening times on different days)*
- **Jedburgh** Murray's Green, Jedburgh, TD8 6BE tel: 01835 863170 *Open All Year*
- **Kelso** Town House, The Square, Kelso, TD5 7HF tel: 01573 228055 *Open All Year*
- **Melrose** Abbey House, Abbey Street, TD6 9LG tel: 01896 822283 *Open All Year*
- **Peebles** 23 High Street, Peebles, EH45 8AG tel: 01721 723159 *Open All Year*
- **Selkirk** Halliwells House, Selkirk, TD7 4BL tel: 01750 20054 *Seasonal Openings (20 Mar - 31 Oct)*

Dumfries & Galloway
www.visitdumfriesandgalloway.co.uk

- **Castle Douglas** Market Hill Car Park, Castle Douglas, DG7 1AE tel: 01556 502611 Seasonal Openings *(20 Mar - 31 Oct, Open Bank Holiday Sundays only)*
- **Dumfries** 64 Whitesands, Dumfries DG1 2RS tel: 01387 253862 *Open All Year (Open Bank Holiday Sundays only)*
- **Gretna** Unit 38, Gretna Gateway Outlet Village, Glasgow Road, Gretna, DG16 5GG tel: 01461 337834 *Open All Year*
- **Kirkcudbright** Harbour Square, Kirkcudbright DG6 4HY tel: 01557 330494 *Open All Year (closed Dec - mid Feb)*
- **Moffat** 3 Churchgate, Moffat, DG10 9JU tel: 01683 220620 *Seasonal Openings (20 Mar - 31 Oct, Open Bank Holiday Sundays only)*
- **Newton Stewart** Dashwood Square, Newton Stewart DG10 9JU tel: 01671 402431 *Seasonal Openings (20 Mar – 31 Oct, Open Bank Holiday Sundays only)*
- **Southwaite** M6 Service Area, Southwaite, CA4 0NS tel: 01697 473445 *Open All Year*
- **Stranraer** Burns House, 28 Harbour Street, Stranraer, Dumfries DG9 7RA tel: 01776 702595 *Open All Year (Open Bank Holiday Sundays only)*

Edinburgh & Lothians
www.edinburgh.org

- **Dunbar** 141 High Street, Dunbar, EH42 1ES tel: 01368 863353 *Seasonal Openings*
- **Edinburgh** Princes Mall, 3 Princes Street, Edinburgh, EH2 2QP tel: 0131 473 3820 *Open All Year*
- **Edinburgh Airport** Main Concourse, Edinburgh International Airport, EH12 9DN tel: 0131 344 3299 *Open All Year*
- **Linlithgow** County Buildings, High Street, Linlithgow. tel: 01506 775320 *Seasonal Openings (1 Apr - 30 Sept)*
- **Newtongrange** Scottish Mining Museum, Newtongrange, EH22 4QN tel: 0131 663 4262 *Seasonal Openings*
- **North Berwick** 1 Quality Street, North Berwick, EH39 4HJ tel: 01620 892197 *Open All Year*

Glasgow & the Clyde Valley
www.visitscotland.com/citybreaks

- **Abington** Welcome Break, Motorway Service Area, Junction 13, M74 Abington, ML12 6RG tel: 01864 502436 *Open All Year*
- **Biggar** 155 High Street, Biggar, ML12 6DI tel: 01899 221066 *Seasonal Openings*
- **Glasgow** 11 George Square, Glasgow G2 1DY tel: 0141 204 4400 *Open All Year*
- **Glasgow Airport** International Arrivals Hall, Glasgow International Airport, PA3 2ST tel: 0141 848 4440 *Open All Year*
- **Lanark** Horsemarket, Ladyacre Road, Lanark, ML11 7QI tel: 01555 661661 *Open All Year*
- **Paisley** 9A Gilmour Street, Paisley, PA1 1DD tel: 0141 889 0711 *Open All Year*

Highlands & Skye
www.visithighlands.com

- **Aviemore** Grampian Road, Aviemore, PH22 1PP tel: 01479 810930 *Open All Year*
- **Daviot Wood** Picnic Area (A9), Daviot Wood, by Inverness, IV1 2ER tel: 01463 772203 *Seasonal Openings (21 Mar - 25 Oct)*
- **Drumnadrochit** The Car Park, Drumnadrochit, Inverness-shire, IV63 6TX tel: 01456 459086 *Open All Year*
- **Dufftown** The Clock Tower, The Square, Dufftown, AB55 4AD tel: 01340 820501 *Open All Year*
- **Dunvegan** 2 Lochside, Dunvegan, Isle of Skye, IV55 8WB tel: 01470 521581 *Open All Year*
- **Durness** Sangomore, Durness, IV27 4PZ tel: 01971 511259 *Seasonal Openings (1 Mar - 25 Oct)*
- **Elgin** 17 High Street, Elgin, IV30 1EG tel: 01343 542666 *Open All Year*
- **Fort William** 15 High Street, Fort William, PH33 6DH tel: 01397 701801 *Open All Year*
- **Grantown-on-Spey** 54 High Street, Grantown on Spey, PH26 3EH tel: 01479 872773 *Seasonal Openings (17 Mar - 25 Oct)*
- **Inverness** Castle Wynd, Inverness, IV2 3BJ tel: 01463 252401 *Open All Year*
- **Lochinver** Assynt, Kirk Lane, Lochinver, IV27 4LT tel: 01571 844330 *Seasonal Openings (17 Mar - 25 Oct)*
- **Portree** Bayfield Road, Portree, Isle of Skye, IV51 9EL tel: 01478 614906 *Open All Year*
- **Ullapool** 6 Argyll Street, Ullapool, Ross-shire, IV26 2UB tel: 01854 612486 *Seasonal Openings (17 Mar - 25 Oct)*
- **Thurso** Riverside Road, Thurso, KW14 8BU tel: 01847 892371 *Seasonal Openings (21 Mar - 25 Oct)*

FRESH SEAFOOD IN CRAIL

WILDLIFE BOAT TRIP, LOCH TORRIDON

The Kingdom of Fife
www.visitfife.com

- **Anstruther** Scottish Fisheries Museum, Harbourhead, Anstruther, KY10 3AB tel: 01333 311073 *Seasonal Openings (21 Mar - 26 Oct)*
- **Crail** Crail Museum, 62 Marketgate, Crail, KY10 3TL tel: 01333 450859 *Seasonal Openings (21 Mar - 30 Sept)*
- **Dunfermline** 1 High Street, Dunfermline, KY12 7DL tel: 01383 720999 *Open All year*
- **Kirkcaldy** The Merchant's House, 339 High Street, Kirkcaldy, KY1 1JL tel: 01592 267775 *Open All year*
- **St. Andrews** 70 Market Street, St. Andrews, KY16 9NU tel: 01334 472021 *Open All year*

Orkney
www.visitorkney.com

- **Kirkwall** The Travel Centre, West Castle St, Kirkwall,Orkney, KW15 1GU tel: 01856 872856 *Open All Year*
- **Stromness** Ferry Terminal Building, Pier Head, Stromness, Orkney, KW16 3AA tel: 01856 850716 *Seasonal Openings (17 Mar - 25 Oct)*

The Outer Hebrides
www.visitthebrides.com

- **Castlebay** Main Street, Castlebay, Isle of Barra, HS9 5XD tel: 01871 810336 *Seasonal Openings (20 Mar - 18 Oct)*
- **Lochboilsdale** Pier Road, Isle of South Uist, HS8 5TH tel: 01878 700286 *Seasonal Openings*
- **Stornoway** 26 Cromwell Street, Stornoway, Isle of Lewis, HS1 2DD tel: 01851 703088 *Open All Year*

Perthshire
www.perthshire.co.uk

- **Aberfeldy** The Square, Aberfeldy, PH15 2DD tel: 01887 820276 *Open All Year*
- **Blairgowrie** 26 Wellmeadow, Blairgowrie PH10 6AS tel: 01250 872960 *Open All Year*
- **Crieff** High Street, Crieff, PH7 3HU tel: 01764 652578 *Open All Year*
- **Dunkeld** The Cross, Dunkeld, PH8 0AN tel: 01350 727688 *Open All Year*
- **Kinross** 27 High street, Kinross, KY13 8AP tel: 01577 863680 Seasonal Openings (31 Mar - 28 Sept)
- **Perth** Lower City Mills, West Mill Street, Perth, PH1 5QP tel: 01738 450600 *Open All Year*
- **Pitlochry** 22 Atholl Road, Pitlochry, PH16 5BX tel: 01796 472215 *Open All Year*

Shetland
www.visitshetland.com

- **Lerwick** Market Cross, Lerwick, Shetland, ZE1 0LU tel: 01595 693434 *Open All Year*
- **Sumburgh (Airport)** Wilsness Terminal, Sumburgh Airport, Shetland ZE3 9JP tel: 01595 693434 *Open All Year*

Canoeing on Loch Tay

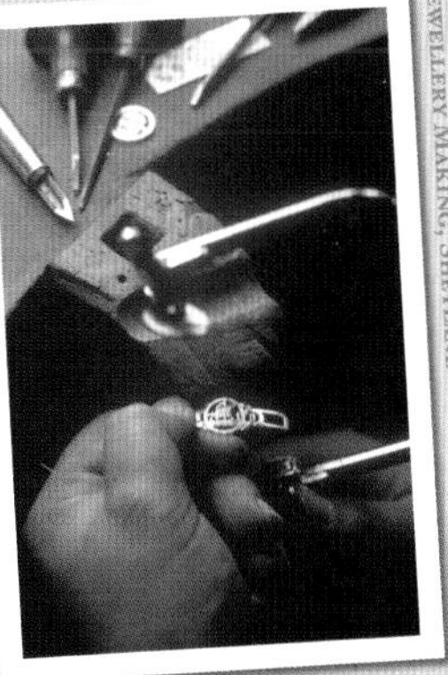

Jewellery Making, Shetland

Whisky to be won

The Great Visitor Information Centre Trail

IF *you are one of the first 50 people to visit 5 Visitor Information Centres, you'll be rewarded for working up a thirst by receiving a bottle of The Glenrothes Select Reserve.*

As Speyside's best kept secret, The Glenrothes is a hand-crafted single malt whisky we're sure you'll love. Every time you visit a Visitor Information Centre, just get the page opposite stamped with each centre's unique stamp and then send the page (just carefully tear it out) to us at: ***Secret Scotland/Glenrothes, Freepost GW 8625, Dunoon, Argyll, PA23 8ZZ.*** *Remember to include your name and address.*

Happy travels!

DRINKAWARE.CO.UK
Enjoy Scotland (and The Glenrothes) responsibly.
www.theglenrothes.com

Open to UK residents aged over 18 years only. Promotion ends 31st December 2009, or while stocks last. There are 50 bottles to be claimed. Each Visitor Information Centre has its unique stamp. No photocopies accepted. Only one bottle per household.

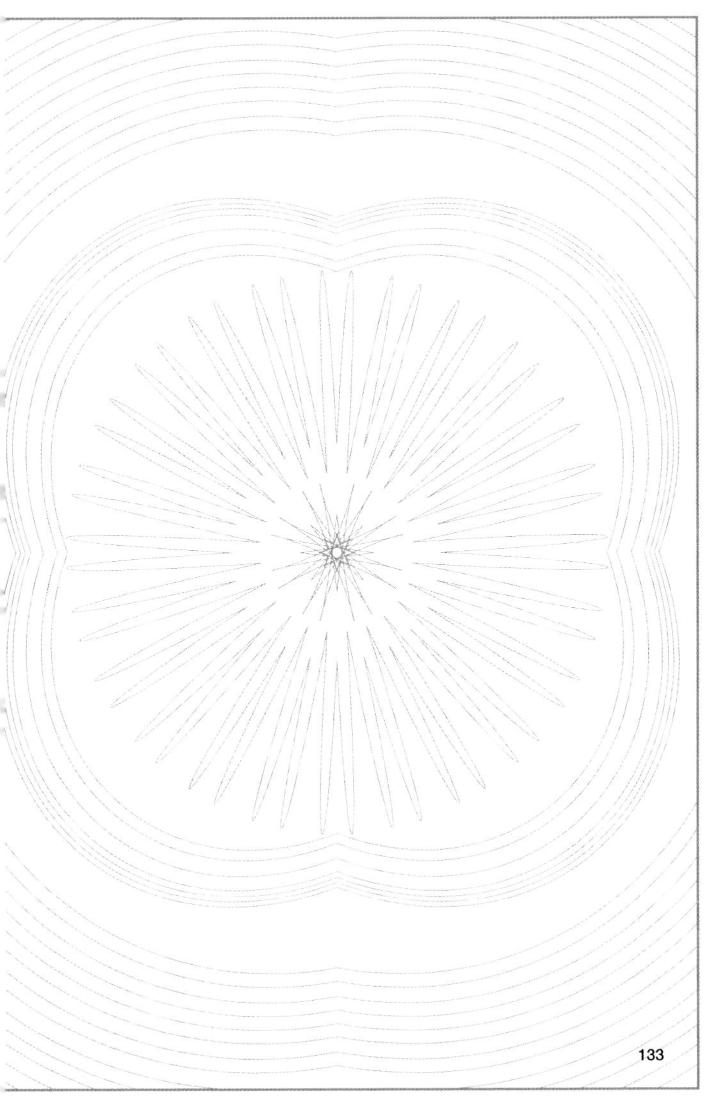

Notes

Use this space to keep your own notes

Notes